O N   T H E
RACK

ON THE
RACK

DAVID GOWER
with Alan Lee

Stanley Paul

LONDON · SYDNEY · AUCKLAND · JOHANNESBURG

Stanley Paul & Co. Ltd

An imprint of Random Century Group Ltd
20 Vauxhall Bridge Road, London SW1V 2SA

Random Century Australia (Pty) Ltd
20 Alfred Street, Milsons Point, Sydney 2061

Random Century New Zealand Limited
PO Box 40-086, Glenfield, Auckland 10

Century Hutchinson South Africa (Pty) Ltd
PO Box 337, Bergvlei 2012, South Africa

First published 1990

Set in Rockwell Light & Helvetica Normal
by SX Composing Ltd, Rayleigh, Essex
Printed and bound in Great Britain by
Butler & Tanner, Frome and London

British Library Cataloguing in Publication Data
Gower, David
  On the rack.
  1. Cricket. English teams. Test matches
  I. Title II. Lee, Alan, *1954-*
  796.35865

ISBN 0 09 174541 1

Contents

Acknowledgements

The author and publishers would like to thank Patrick Eagar, Graham Morris and AllSport for supplying the photographs in this book.

CHAPTER ONE

'The Committee Decision'

Time, they say, can heal all wounds. I have been giving the theory plenty of practice. Nobody with a sense of self-respect can escape the hurt of failure in a public position. Nobody who has captained his country can enjoy the pain which comes with rejection. Well, it has now happened to me twice.

For almost three years, since first falling from grace in 1986, I had scarcely given the job a thought. There had simply been no point so long as Peter May, the man who dismissed me, remained in power. But suddenly, in the spring of 1989, things changed. Looking back now, it might have been better for my peace of mind if they had stayed exactly as they were.

When Ted Dexter took over as chairman of the newly formed England committee and, by inference, as chairman of selectors, the name of D. Gower was evidently retrieved from the waste-bin of discarded captains and restored to the list of prime contenders. Within weeks, I was back in charge. But the process by which it now transpires I was appointed, the tortured summer in hapless pursuit of the Ashes, and the handover of both my job and my place in the team, conspired to make up a period which did little for my dignity and nothing at all for my tranquility. Delighted though I was to be given a second chance as captain, there were times when I questioned if it was all worthwhile and I am now profoundly glad it is over.

I hardly knew Ted before his appointment brought our orbits into collision, but I knew of him as a communicator and that encouraged me to believe the relationship might work in a way that it had never done between Peter May and me. We simply were not on the same wavelength. PBH, as he is universally known, had, it is true, nominated me for office when Bob Willis retired in 1984. He showed me ample support that year, when we lost 5 – 0 to the West Indies, and gave me the chance to go to India and redeem myself. While we were winning there, and against Australia the following summer, all was well, but after our next drubbing by the West Indies, on the 1986 tour, I felt my days were numbered. Our relationship was largely professional, revolving around selection meetings and little else, and the manner in which he terminated my tenure, at Lord's in 1986, left little scope for pondering the prospects of ever working together again.

Ted, I sensed, was very different. From the start I saw in him the possibility of a kindred spirit and, despite the unfortunate way things worked out, I still maintain I was right. I have a certain admiration for the way he played his cricket and the way he has lived his life. Ted has always been an adventurer, and if people see a little of him in me, I would happily agree. Our only personal contact, before working together, had been the odd occasion when he offered me technical advice on my batting. There are any number of former players trading in this commodity but many need regarding with suspicion as they are motivated by profit, ego, and sometimes both. Ted, I felt at the time, was entirely genuine. He believed he could help me and he did it in a style which was neither intrusive nor patronising. I liked him for that.

In Ted Dexter, pictured here with the TCCB's chief executive Alan Smith, I sensed a kindred spirit, and still maintain I was right

I suppose I might have guessed what was to come when Ted volunteered some pretty flattering comments about me and my image, even before his own appointment had been made official. But I didn't. It was not that the captaincy failed to interest me; on the contrary, I had reached a stage in my career where an additional motivation was desirable, if not essential. The truth is that I had long ago put all thoughts about the job out of my head, not to be revived until and unless someone told me to my face that I was back in the game.

That morning arrived one day towards the end of March. Ted himself telephoned me and asked if I would motor down to his house on the following Sunday to discuss the vacant captaincy. Ted lives in Ealing, west London, and he suggested I should be there by 4 p.m. Punctuality may not always be my most reliable virtue, but I made sure I was right on time for this engagement. It was the nearest thing, I reasoned, to a job interview, and if you wanted the job you were wise not to put yourself out of the running by turning up late for the interview.

Ted was not conducting proceedings alone. Also present was Micky Stewart – a slight surprise on the day but a logical addition to the interview board because, as England manager, he would have to work very closely with the new captain. What followed was two hours of informal discussion, with unmistakably serious undertones. It might sound amusing, for instance, to be quizzed about any skeletons I may have in my cupboard, but the motive behind the question was no joke. It is a sad fact of modern sporting life that those who aspire to prominent positions can expect no respite from the attentions of the media, even extending to the history of their private lives. Unfair it may be, but that does not constitute an excuse for ignoring the possibilities; Ted has worked for a tabloid newspaper and knows the score. I think I was able to reassure him.

I had braced myself to be asked about South Africa. It was a question which had to be asked; there was little point in nominating a captain who was planning to abandon ship at the first offer of a caseload of rand. I gave the honest answer that going to South Africa would, in my view, be an admission of impending retirement – something I did not intend to contemplate just yet.

When I left the house I was not totally sure of how well I had stated my case, but at least felt happy that my responses had been honest and positive. I had no real idea what impresssion I had left, but ten days later the matter was apparently resolved. Ted phoned my home to offer me the position for the entire summer against Australia.

I don't think either of us wasted a moment worrying about whether I would accept, and in the genuine excitement of the moment I did not give another thought to the rumour I had heard, some days earlier, that Mike Gatting had got the job. Had I done so, I would doubtless have reflected that the cricket grapevine is notoriously misinformed. It was some distance into the summer before I learned that it had been rather more than a rumour; indeed, that certain revealing facts had been kept from me.

Mike Gatting was born only two months after me, in June 1957, and our careers have been linked by a variety of events and parallels. Although he had lost the England captaincy under curious circumstances the previous summer, I had no doubt that he was one of those being considered now. In fact, I assumed that it was a three-sided contest and it was only much later that I discovered Graham Gooch had not even been interviewed. Ted and Micky, it seems, had rapidly narrowed the field to two.

Each of us, of course, had done the job before, and each had experienced a share of success. First time around, I had won in India and at home against Australia; Mike had led the team which achieved such comprehensive success in Australia in 1986 – 87. Now, at the beginning of 1989, both of us were keen to do it again. Oddly, it could be thought that both of us emerged from the episode as losers. Mike's reappointment was vetoed at top level and he took his grievances off to South Africa; I got the job – unknown to me as second choice – but then supervised a season which degenerated into a shambles for the team and, more specifically, for me.

Mike evidently knew the circumstances of the job appointment. It can only be a matter of guesswork for me as to how he found out, because nobody ever told me the facts of the matter and I never discussed it with Mike. This may seem strange to those who see us as close contemporaries but, although we have got along well over all the years I have known him, our relationship has not been one of shared confidences.

My close friends in the game, those whom I might seek out for food, wine and social company, are few. Allan Lamb, Chris Cowdrey and Graham Gooch would fit this bill. With 'Gatt' and me, it has tended to be a case of mutual respect first and last, because we are essentially different people. This respect, however, is strong enough to have formed a bond between us. It dates back to the 1984 – 85 tour to India. I was captain; Mike's career was at a crossroads. He had failed persistently and eccentrically against the West Indies the previous summer, when everyone remembers him out twice in a

match padding up to Malcolm Marshall. He had not made a century in Test cricket although he had been given plenty of chances. He was far from certain to be chosen for the tour.

When the selectors met, I was adamant that he should not only be included but should be my vice-captain. There was some opposition but I won the point, with well-chronicled results. Mike's long wait ended with a century in Bombay; he then made a double-century in Madras. We won the series and his career had at long last taken off.

I know that my loyalty to Mike did not go unappreciated. I also know that he was acutely embarrassed eighteen months later when Peter May relieved me of the captaincy at the end of the Lord's Test against India and immediately installed Mike in my place. It was a messy handover and Mike did not know what to do or say. For someone who had just been handed the biggest job in cricket, he looked remarkably miserable. For the next few weeks he still called me 'captain' purely out of long habit. Gradually, though, he came to terms with the situation and worked tremendously hard at the job. By the end of that summer he was demonstrably in charge and the team was functioning well, but it was not until we got to Australia that the change was complete.

Mike and Micky Stewart worked well together. They were from similar backgrounds and they tended to see things the same way. In this regime, it was soon clear, there was no scope for any contribution from me. John Emburey was promoted to vice-captain on tour and the first few weeks of that trip were some of the roughest I have known. All my connections with the business end of the ship had been severed and it did nothing for my pride and self-esteem.

As captain, Mike did certain things better than me. He was more adept at dealing with the new, young players and would spend more time working with them. Our styles of leadership, in fact, were different in many ways; Mike was much more the up-and-at-them type, bustling about, clapping his hands, slapping backs and barking orders. By contrast, I suppose my approach looked very low-key, but I do not believe that necessarily made it less effective.

I was not available for the fateful tour of Pakistan which doubtless contributed more than any barmaid to Mike losing the job. I observed the controversial incidents like anyone else back in England – on television and in the newspapers – and while I appreciate the players' view that no one who was not there can possibly know what it was like, the sense of detachment arguably allowed a more rational judgement.

Previous trips to the sub-continent had taught me all I needed to know about their umpiring standards and the strain they could place upon a touring team. Sometimes, within the siege mentality of a struggling, suffering team, it can all seem like some evil conspiracy. So I did have some sympathy for Mike; he probably felt he could not win, would not be allowed to win. Having said that much in mitigation, I must still be critical of him because there is only one way of defusing the type of situation which confronted him in Faisalabad and it is not by shouting at an umpire while belligerently wagging a finger in his face. I hope I would never have allowed myself to do that and I am sure Mike knows, in hindsight, how unforgivable it was for England's captain to behave in such a way, especially in the eyes of many of those in authority.

It was, however, quite another thing to be dismissed for the fanciful muck-raking of a tabloid newspaper. Mike openly resented it and, it seems, was unprepared to put the affair behind him and get on with his international career. It lurked in his mind, affecting his appetite for Test cricket and, eventually perhaps, his entire perception of the future. He went to South Africa, in my view, for all the wrong reasons. It must have played on his mind that things might have been very different. For it has since transpired, of course, that Mike, and not I, would have been the captain against Australia last summer but for the application of a new and little-known veto.

I had always been prepared to discover that Micky Stewart had wanted 'Gatt' as captain. I would have been surprised had it been otherwise. But Ted was different. The media had publicly marked him out as a Gower man and I saw no reason to doubt the matter. It appears we were wrong because, by the time it came to the England committee meeting which was to decide the captaincy, Ted had reportedly lined up alongside Micky in support of the Gatting nomination.

There are two others on the committee but with the chairman usually assumed to have the casting vote, Mike would have been appointed but for the intervention of Ossie Wheatley. Mr Wheatley is chairman of the cricket sub-committee on the Test and County Cricket Board. It is an influential position, though for some months – indeed, until the season had been laid to rest – precious few people knew quite how influential he had been.

The veto facility had been agreed by the Board only a few months earlier. It was invested in the chairman of cricket and had been designed, apparently, largely to prevent any politically provocative appointments. Mr Wheatley applied it to Gatting because, as he later explained, he felt it would be 'insensitively premature' to bring him back to the job so soon after the well-documented controversies. With their nomination blocked, Ted and Micky evidently agreed upon me as a substitute. It was also agreed, though at whose suggestion I have no idea, that I would not be told the procedure by which I had come into the job. Leaving aside the rights and wrongs of the veto, which is really not my province, I feel entitled to question whether I should have been told. As we have since discovered, it was never likely to remain a secret indefinitely.

A version of events reached my ears a few weeks into the season. Again, it came down the grapevine. Again, I paid little attention. 'So what?' about sums up my reaction. After all, I was captain, by whatever means, and I could not at the time see that it made much difference how many committee members had voted for me. To pursue the story would, in any case, have distracted me from my aims at a time when I was feeling positive about life in general and the captaincy in particular.

There were psychologically negative implications to knowing that I had been the second choice. The fact is that the news had given me more of a boost than I could have expected. I did not wish to ruin that, so I ignored what I had heard and got on with the job. By the end of the season, however, I could see that it had not been a very tenable position for me. However much support I had apparently received from Ted and Micky in public, privately there was ample scope to suspect that if things went wrong, I would be on my own.

Almost the first duty of anyone elected to a public position, it seems, is to give a press conference. This I duly did, amid the musty, mid-winter memories of the Lord's Long Room, on the afternoon of Wednesday 5 April. In thinking back over that conference, where faces familiar to me among the cricketing media were almost lost among the forest of microphones and TV cameras, one particular moment sticks in my mind. Ted Dexter, seated alongside me behind the polished oak table, was asked, quite legitimately, whether I had been the unanimous choice as captain. Ted is carefully precise with words, and his answer, repeated under cross-examination, was that it had been 'the decision of the full England committee', phraseology from which he would not be moved. Although this was plainly a case of dodging a difficult issue, I was too concerned with the things I wished to say myself to be disturbed by what I had heard. If it made any impression on me at all, it would merely have been a subconscious noting that Micky must, as I suspected, have voted for 'Gatt'.

I was pretty wound up before the conference. I am not blind to the importance of this part of the job and I was very anxious to create the right impression from the start. Plenty of people are still willing to dismiss me as a dilettante, unsuited to the demands of leadership, and I did not want to start off casually, as if I was just drifting into the job. I was deliberately positive, firm and enthusiastic but tried, at the same time, to retain my sense of

14

Beneath the royal portrait, Ted tells the gathered media that my appointment was 'the decision of the full England committee'

humour. It is precious to me, although I know that at times it can all too easily be misinterpreted as facetiousness.

In general, the conference was good-natured and optimistic. There was evidently a widespread sense that an overdue fresh start had been made. It was, of course, a honeymoon period between the media and the new men in charge. I was worldly enough about such relationships to avoid the mistake of believing things would always be so chummy. I could not, however, have anticipated quite how seriously things would deteriorate during the subsequent months – to a point where I tried hard, although in vain, to disassociate myself from the David Gower being written about, simply to salvage some peace of mind.

As the scheduled winter tour or India had been a victim of politics, it was a long time since any England squad had been together. An early gathering, at which both Ted and I could supplement the practice facility with a few well-chosen words about aims and ambitions, was clearly a sound idea. It came about on 13 April, barely a week after my appointment had been confirmed. A selected group of players, made up largely of those who would have toured India, convened at Lord's with the intention of using the nets at the Nursery End. The weather scuppered that idea, however, and the day's programme was restricted to another press conference – this time with rather less to say – a promotional lunch and an afternoon workout in the indoor nets.

I have certain reservations about the value of indoor practice, but this was not a wasted day. Simply getting the players together at this time of year was an advance on anything previously achieved and I sensed a genuine atmosphere of anticipation, which Ted's high-profile enthusiasm had done much to generate.

During the press conference, held in a room behind the ground's main grandstand scoreboard, I was asked for my views on the Australian tourists. It was mischievously put to me that the coming series was a 'relegation issue' in the Test nations' league table. I said that I was paying no heed to all the denigratory things being written about the supposed state of the game in both Australia and England. I believed there would be two well-matched and competitive teams, the only difference being that we held the Ashes and meant to keep them. It was possibly a touch jingoistic, but I reasoned it would do no harm to bang the drum now and again.

If we were to retain the Ashes – and I genuinely felt we could at that stage – I certainly felt there was an important role in the operation for Mike Gatting. We had still not spoken about the captaincy decision, and while I fully expected him to be disappointed, I saw no reason why he should not

(*top*) My aim was to be positive from the outset, beginning with my first press conference at Lord's in April

(*left*) The toss before the start of the Texaco Trophy one-day series

(*above*) Our one prize of the summer ... the Texaco Trophy

(*right*) Headingley – down but still optimistic

(*below*) Alderman persistently troubled Graham Gooch and, at Headingley, dismissed him lbw for the first of several times

(*bottom*) Bowled by Geoff Lawson for 57 in the first innings of the Lord's Test. My expression says it all

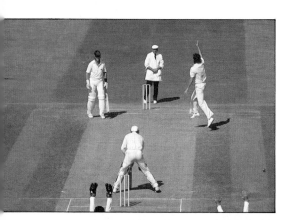

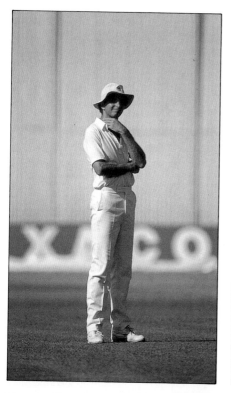

(*top left*) Wondering how to stop Taylor – or was it Waugh, or Jones, or Marsh?

(*top right*) Ted Dexter reveals details of South African defections and reaffirms his support of my position – Manchester

(*above*) The Australians celebrate another Gooch failure. After this match, at Old Trafford, he offered to stand down

(*top left*) In the nets at Trent Bridge prior to the Fifth Test

(*top right*) Delight at catching Steve Waugh for nought. Unfortunately, this only reduced Australia to 553 for five

(*left*) Allan Border in charge in all senses at Trent Bridge

(*above*) Gladstone Small, a genuine quality bowler, takes the new ball in the final Test at The Oval

reclaim his place in the team and make a lot of runs. He had a prior lunch commitment on the day the squad gathered and had phoned to ask if he could miss our own function and arrive in time for the afternoon nets. I willingly agreed. It might have been different if one of the younger, inexperienced players had made a similar request, but I have never gone along with the theory that every member of a team should be treated alike. Players such as Mike and Ian Botham have accomplished so much over the years that they must, I believe, be allowed a certain leeway and not viewed as clones of some mythical stereotype.

My other duty on that April afternoon was to establish the terms of my relationship with the team manager. Micky Stewart and I had not previously worked together in this way and I felt some job specification was necessary.

'Gatt' was always very happy to give the manager his head in many areas; I suspect it was much the same with the three other captains who succeeded him during 1988, if only because each of them was feeling his way. I was in a more fortunate position – appointed for the full summer and able to take a more positive, long-term line on the way I felt things should be done. Basically, I remain a traditionalist who believes that the captain should run the team in his own way.

Micky and I had a chat at the end of the day. I told him that I would appreciate his support behind the scenes but that I wanted to lead proceedings in respect of policies, team talks and tactics. It meant, inevitably, that Micky would have a lower profile and I don't suppose he was especially happy with that.

Just once, during the summer, Ted made a token intervention. It was at the Benson and Hedges Cup final in July, where I was doing some radio commentary. We had already played three Tests by then, losing two of them, and when we met up in the Lord's pavilion Ted made a point of suggesting I might use Micky more as a sounding post. I appreciated, and always have done, that certain aspects of a game are better observed from the balcony than out in the middle, but the successful trading of such information relies on a rapport between captain and manager which, in this series, did not burgeon that much, despite the chairman's intervention. I am sure this was only because Micky and I are not exactly out of the same mould and were always going to approach things differently, but the intention was always there to maintain an equable working pattern for the sake of all concerned.

By imposing my authority on the situation, I was also very aware that I was taking a risk. There could be no passing the buck in the event of heavy defeat. I had set the terms. I would have to take the blame.

I had no such thoughts in my head, however, during the early days of the season. I don't think I realised how much I wanted another chance in the captaincy until I actually got it. It gave me an incalculable boost, so that I even approached the dubious prospect of county cricket under three sweaters in late April with an unaccustomed spring in my step.

This manifested itself in a score of 228 for Leicestershire against Glamorgan on Saturday 22 April. It was the biggest score of my career. Until then, my best effort had been in a Test Match against Australia, of which I was quietly proud. If the record-book entry does not now look so glamorous, this was still an innings which delighted me because it accurately reflected the way I was feeling. There have been many times when I have found it difficult to motivate myself for a county game, but despite the bitterly cold weather and the apology for a crowd at my home ground of Grace Road, there was not a problem at any stage of this day. I passed my previous highest score for Leicestershire by a considerable distance and assuaged the pangs of conscience I periodically experience over my county contributions.

It might, of course, have been one of those rare and precious days when the ball simply keeps hitting the middle of the bat for no discernible reason, but I preferred to believe it was directly connected with my generally positive outlook on life.

I was back in the big time and unquestionably enjoying it. At the back of my mind lurked the memories of the extra work the captaincy entailed, the nervous energy to be expended and the personal pressure to be borne. But far closer to the forefront of my thoughts than the ignominies I suffered in the Caribbean as captain of the 1986 team which was beaten 5 – 0 were the glories of the 1985 English summer, when we so convincingly beat the previous Australian tourists. I felt a sense of optimism, and the double-century against Glamorgan was statistical confirmation of it. A week later, the Australians landed at Heathrow. My new-found confidence was soon to be put to the test.

CHAPTER TWO

A Winning Tie in the Texaco

One of the best traditions of England tours is that they invariably begin at Arundel. It may not be much preparation for what is to come, nor provide any warning of some of the starker environments in which they have to play, but for a visiting team nothing could be more delightfully English than a Sunday afternoon fixture on the beautiful Castle ground.

The Duchess of Norfolk's XI customarily provide the opposition, and this year, as Leicestershire had no Sunday League fixture, I was able to accept an invitation to captain the side. As I tossed the coin for the first of many times during the summer, with my old friend Allan Border, I remember looking around me and thinking that things could not possibly be so relaxed again.

According to Colin Cowdrey there was a record crowd of 10,000 on a perfect spring day. Sadly, the cricket did not quite match the setting for it was an utterly one-sided match, my team losing by 120 runs and probably being flattered to get so close. Although there would be far more serious occasions on which to judge them, the Australians already looked in ominously good order, particularly with the bat, and some of those who had glibly predicted we would wipe the floor with them were hurriedly revising their assessments.

The tourists went off for their series of warm-up games and I returned to Leicester. We were not due to meet up again until the Texaco Trophy series of one-day internationals and it was on 20 May, two weeks after the Arundel game, that I met up with Ted and Micky for our first selection conference of the summer.

I decided to take the initiative and suggested, as soon as the usual preliminaries were out of the way, that I should open the batting in the three limited-overs games. The offer was rapidly accepted; so far so good. Micky said that the same idea had been in his mind anyway, and Ted was apparently content just to rubber-stamp the proposal. This made the rest of the

19

process relatively straightforward because it created space within a thirteen-man squad for all the batsmen we wanted. The bowling did not present great problems, either. We have played the limited-overs game far more effectively than Test cricket in recent years and experience told us that Neil Foster, Phillip DeFreitas, Derek Pringle and John Emburey were all proven experts in this field. Graham Dilley was injured so we included Paul Jarvis of Yorkshire as a fast bowler in good form.

The main discussion concerned Ian Botham. He had been through a very serious back operation but, as is his wont, scoffed heavily at the cynics who said he would never come back. An enormous media group followed him on Worcestershire's pre-season tour to Queensland, his intended comeback, but desperately poor weather ruined that plan and it had to be admitted that he had achieved little since the county season had started. We were picking him more in faith than on any convincing evidence of form, but I had taken the trouble to seek him out a few days before the selection meeting, and even allowing for Ian's natural bravado I came away with the conviction that he still had plenty to offer. His inclusion predictably delighted the tabloid press, who long for such charismatic figures to carry their headlines. It also inspired the general public, although it seemed that no further incentives were needed to get people through the gates. Crowds had turned up in force at all the early tourist games and now, I understood, it was impossible to beg, borrow or steal a ticket for any of the Texaco games.

I have attracted some criticism over the years for openly expressing ambivalence towards one-day cricket in general and a cynicism about the amount of one-day internationals we are obliged to play in certain parts of the world. This is not to say that I consciously permit my standards to drop in these games, rather that they can never stimulate me as a Test match unfailingly does. Limited-overs games invariably fall into a predictable pattern and seldom linger in the memory longer than the start of the next one. A good Test match can live in the memory for ever.

With all that said, I was naturally aware that the three fixtures confronting me at the end of May were rather different. If ever overs cricket was designed to mean something above the mundane to me, this was the occasion. So much hot air had been trumpeted about the new England regime before a ball was bowled that there was suddenly an uncomfortably acute pressure to justify public expectations. Fortunately, whatever mishaps were to befall us later, we crossed the first hurdle without falling flat on our faces.

The Texaco Trophy, as it has been known since Prudential handed over their original sponsorship, continues to thrive because it retains a certain rarity value. Whereas in Australia, a touring team may play ten or more one-day internationals, and in other countries at least five, the English authorities have persisted with a sensible ration. Each Texaco series comprises just three games, or two in the years when we entertain two tours. By playing the three games consecutively, over a five-day period, public interest is captured and held, and although there are those who believe the Trophy would be better sited at the end of the season, as it once was, I am a believer in playing the one-day cricket first, rather as a light appetiser. Having more than once reached the weary end of a daunting, mentally draining six-Test series in Australia to be confronted by an apparently endless programme of anti-climactic limited-overs games, I feel well qualified in this matter!

Although we have yet to win a World Cup, the ultimate in overs cricket, England's record at the instant game has been pretty impressive in recent years. We have beaten everyone, including the West Indies, and while this form has never translated to Test cricket, it is unarguably better to be successful at something than nothing. It was Australia who beat us in the final of the 1987 World Cup in Calcutta, so there was an extra incentive for wanting to begin the summer well – especially for those who had suffered the disappointment in India. Frankly, I think both teams were very confident. Bob Simpson, the Australian coach who has done much to restore pride in their side, went on record as saying they were the best one-day team in the world. I kept my own counsel on that one but I had no doubt we were capable of winning if we performed to potential.

The first of the games was played at Old Trafford on Thursday 25 May. It was to be here in Manchester, much later in the summer, that Australia would regain the Ashes and I was to experience the most miserable days of my tenure as captain. That, however, was all in the unexplored future as I set off from Leicester on the Wednesday morning for our traditional pre-series net practice.

I was due at the ground by 2 p.m. for a press conference, and I almost didn't make it. The M6 motorway was a nightmare – mile upon mile of nose-to-tail crawl. Not for the first time, I wondered how on earth so many office workers commute vast distances on the roads every day. Covering the last few miles at a speed not guaranteed to find favour with the Greater Manchester Police, I arrived only a few minutes late.

Ted was already holding court to an enormous press contingent in the pavilion, so there was no opportunity for me to discuss diplomacy with him. I joined the chairman and made what I considered to be the right positive remarks about the coming games. I was then asked who would be opening the batting with Graham Gooch, and short of giving a direct answer, I said it would not be a total surprise if he was a left-hander. The scribes had their story, it seemed. It was only later that someone told me how Ted's face had fallen when, as he saw it, I let the cat out of the bag. The chairman subscribes to the 'walls have ears' theory and believes passionately in keeping as much as possible secret from the opposition. We certainly did not fall out over this minor variance, indeed all parties, including the press, were quite amused by the situation. I have always tried to believe that the press need and appreciate most of the correct information available, but if Ted wanted to be slightly more cagey, it was not going to worry me.

Ted apparently liked the element of surprise to be part of our strategy, but all this meant was that I was now more determined to make the plan work.

All of which will help to explain why I felt unusually nervous the following morning. Contrary to popular belief, I am not immune to such an emotion; anyone who feels icy calm as he goes out to bat in a Test match is probably not best prepared for what is to come. But this was different. Not a Test match, maybe, but the start of what I passionately hoped would be something good and lasting in my career. I badly wanted it to be a good start – and it was.

The Old Trafford pitch, when we inspected it an hour before the game, was not particularly hard and had a detectable tinge of green to it. I listened quietly to the instinctive reaction of a lot of our players that we should bowl first to exploit any early life. Then I reflected alone and decided we should bat. The coin fell in my favour, we did bat and we dominated the game throughout. Graham and I put on 55 in only 12 overs for the first wicket. I made 36 of them and considered that to be a satisfactory start for the experiment. We won the game by 95 runs and that did not flatter us at all. I am sure the Australians must have been dismayed at the way they played but, while not kidding myself that they could do no better, I preferred to concentrate on the positive aspects of our own performance. There were many of them, and I toasted as much over a glass or two of something acceptable in Manchester that evening.

As usual during these series, the team stayed on in Manchester for the night after the game and then, the following morning, we drove down to Nottingham, venue for the second match on the Saturday. This was to be an altogether more competitive contest, with a dramatic, confusing climax which resulted in England 'winning' the game despite the scores finishing level.

I often think that a redeeming feature of one-day cricket is to be the fielding captain during the final overs of a tight game. The tension becomes an enjoyable challenge and the need for constant mental arithmetic sometimes extends to making an outright guess or two. It is gratifying when the guesses produce results, as, to a degree, they did here. The upshot was that

The idea of opening the batting in the one-day series was a good positive start to the summer, and shots like this vindicated the decision

we had effectively won the Texaco Trophy despite standing at 1 – 0 with one to play, because if the Australians were to win the final game the tie-breaker rule would be invoked and the Trent Bridge game awarded to us for having lost fewer wickets. It is doubtful whether many people at Trent Bridge were aware of the small print of the rules during the excitement of the finale. I was, though, and I had it in mind throughout that a tie was almost as good as a win.

The penultimate over contained an element of farce, though with a controversial undercurrent. Ian Healy, the Australian wicket-keeper and by no means a negligible batsman, had been limping heavily on a knee strain, though still raising a very fair gallop whenever necessary. Eventually, midway through the 54th over and with the game balanced precariously, he elected to call for a runner. Dean Jones, one of the fastest men on either side, was sent out. All perfectly fair and within the rules. What happened next, however, was pure chaos. With his runner stationed at square leg, Healy hit the next ball so well that he forgot himself completely and instead of resting on his bat and letting his 'helper' do the donkey work, he sprinted two runs quicker than the bemused Jones.

RIGHT: Ian Healy trying to explain how, though injured, he managed to win the race against his runner, Dean Jones

ABOVE: 'Thanks for popping in.' Dean Jones returns to the pavilion, leaving Healy to run for himself

The umpires, who included the fretting figure of H. D. 'Dickie' Bird, were
visibly perplexed as they moved to confer. I strolled across and suggested
that it now appeared the runner was not needed. The umpires quickly
agreed and Jones was asked to leave the field. He took it all in good part
and I ran across to offer a light-hearted remark about how nice it had been
of him to pop in, but I later learned that the Australian management was no-
where near as sanguine about the matter.

Both Bob Simpson and Allan Border thought it was unfair on an obviously
injured player and, at least by inference, criticised my part in banishing the
runner. Border, in fact, was so transparently upset that one or two journalists
phoned me the following morning to tell me I was in danger of having fallen
out with a man I had long regarded as a friend. I sought him out during the
final match at Lord's, by which time he was viewing it all more dis-
passionately, but it was clearly one of those instances in which the Laws of
the game are not explicit and the umpires have to exercise a judgement. I
am content that anything I said or did was not designed to take an unfair
advantage but to prevent what I considered an unnecessary complication.

Anyway, with all that out of the way, we still faced a decisive last over.
Australia, who had set off with a target of 227 after a typical Allan Lamb
century, had managed 220 of them. Seven from six balls was their target –
and they had already lost too many wickets to profit from the tie. Phillip

BELOW: *I would have loved to have seen a side-on replay, but Ian Healy successfully scampered the leg-bye that tied the second one-day international*

RIGHT: *Australia saw their win at Lord's as rather more than token consolation. Geoff Marsh made a century, Steve Waugh's hitting settled the game and, suddenly, they were a confident unit*

DeFreitas was entrusted with the ball and you can imagine my dismay when he began the over with a 'wide' – unforgivable in such circumstances. His next four balls were all legitimate and four further runs resulted. I then had it in my head that Australia needed only one run from two balls to win, and accordingly brought in the field to save the single.

It was a momentary aberration on my part and we might have paid for it; thank heavens it worked in our favour. Tim May, apparently flustered by the increased pressure from the field, aimed an ugly slog at the fifth ball of the over and was bowled. Australia salvaged a tie with a leg-bye from the last ball, with Healy once more demonstrating that his injury did not prevent him from moving remarkably fast when the need arose. He only just got home though, and there were those in our team who thought otherwise.

And so, after a quiet Sunday morning at home in Leicester, it was down to London and the hotel most of us still refer to as the Westmoreland even though it now boasts the name 'Hilton Regents Park'. It overlooks Lord's,

which is its greatest virtue as it cuts out the necessity for setting off early to the ground and battling against rush-hour traffic.

Monday morning, and a Bank Holiday – customarily the signal for foul weather, but for a pleasant change, the sun was beating down from a very un-English pure blue sky. It was hot, genuinely hot, by the time we began our exercise routine on the Nursery ground and the ice-cream sellers were already doing a heavy trade. Suntan lotion and shades were the order of the day and Lord's, packed to capacity, was a wonderful sight. The crowd had come regardless of the fact that the series was already decided, and there was an expectant feel to the day. I don't think they went away disappointed.

It was in the corresponding game four years earlier that my first Ashes summer as captain had begun to turn for the better. We had lost the first two Texaco Trophy matches that year, and I had been in wretched form, but we won at Lord's and both Graham Gooch and I made centuries – the prelude to a Test series in which we could do little wrong.

Today, most of the circumstances were very different. The series was won and I did not feel in bad form at all. It was Australia who won the game, in another desperately close finish, but there was one surviving parallel in that 'Goochie' and I both made runs again. I scored 61 in an opening stand of 123, so that plan had worked gratifyingly well, and Graham batted virtually throughout the innings for a personal score of 123. He had suffered some troughs in his career but I was convinced he would be a major run-scorer in the series ahead. I had not, at that stage, reckoned with the stifling influence Terry Alderman was to exert on affairs.

Although Lord's had provided a good batting pitch and the outfield was very quick, I think we all felt that 278 would be enough. But some mis-directed bowling from usually reliable performers proved very costly; so too, in the final analysis, did a catch put down by John Emburey (who misses very few) on the mid-wicket boudary when Steve Waugh had scored only 5. He went on to score a decisive 35, including two consecutive sixes off Neil Foster, and Australia got home in the last over.

I remember thinking at the time that Australia would see the result as rather more than token consolation. Although confident that we had looked the better side over the three games, I could well envisage that Border and Simpson would make much of winning the last of them, encouraging their players to believe in themselves.

Overall, I was happy to win the Texaco, though far from carried away by it. Among the most interesting aspects for me had been the mood in the dressing room, which reflected the theme of a fresh start. Tension was general, extending even to Ian Botham, whose constant chatter and bra-vado had the unmistakable mark of an anxious man. He badly wanted to prove himself again and he probably saw his explosive 25 off just 11 balls at Lord's as just the start. Sadly, it was to prove an isolated high spot in an in-tensely disappointing year for a cricketer who continues to make the game more fun for those around him.

CHAPTER THREE

Fateful Decisions

If the Australians were at all infected with the persecution complexes which can spread damagingly through any team on tour, they might have suspected a sinister English plot behind the staging of the First Cornhill Test match at Headingley. Allan Border, for one, could never quite have banished his bad memories of that incredible, Botham-inspired England comeback on the ground which turned the 1981 series on its head, while several more of the Australians will have recalled starting the 1985 Test programme there and losing a typically low-scoring game by five wickets.

Headingley is haunted by the fear of the unknown. Its pitches, in recent years, have never been uninteresting to bowl upon; indeed, the greatest problem has invariably been extending the Tests there into a fifth day. Both teams go there in the uneasy knowledge that a positive result is almost certain, barring bad weather, and that creates a very special tension.

I am absolutely sure that Australia's players approached this match with some apprehension. It was no different for us. This single game had assumed outlandish importance in the scheme of things, both because of the natural desire to draw first blood and because of the pressing public anticipation. It had the potential to dictate the series and, in effect, so it did. We lost the match so conclusively, our second innings surviving for less than four hours on the final afternoon, that Australia went away from Leeds with incalculable psychological gains that we were never able to retrieve.

It could be claimed that the game was won and lost on that fifth day, and it certainly remains a mystery how we managed to give it away, but I am not afraid to say that I personally contributed to the defeat even before the game had begun. I should have known better but, in common with many captains before me, I made two vital decisions on the basis of some hypothetical, fatalistic talk about the weather. Even by the close of that depressing Thursday, I feared I was destined to spend the rest of the match, if not the series, wondering why on earth I had done it.

The decisions were to play an all-seam attack, and to put Australia in to bat. One inevitably followed the other, but both were ill-conceived. My instincts told me as much after only a couple of hours' cricket and by the end of the opening day, with Australia 207 for 3 and the prospect of several further sessions in the field confronting us, I knew the worst. We had made a potentially costly mistake and I fully expected the fact to be drummed home in the following morning's papers. In that, I was not disappointed. After all the waiting, all the heady build-up, it was an intensely deflating way to begin my first Test back in charge.

The maddening part of it is that I had personally been in little doubt, from the time the team was chosen the previous Friday, that we should include the off-spin of John Emburey in our final line-up. It made sense from every angle. I am never in favour of beginning a match with a bowling attack which gives you no options, and even at Headingley, with its well-merited reputation for helping the seamer, I can recall situations when the quicker bowlers failed or flagged and something different was required. Take 1985, for example – it was none other than Emburey himself who took five Australian wickets in the second innings to set up our victory.

Hindsight being so convenient, it now seems perfectly obvious that Emburey should have played and that, given the choice, we should have batted first. We got it wrong because I allowed myself to be swayed. We got things wrong because we tried, collectively, to be too clever when what was called for was conventional simplicity of thinking.

Right up to the morning of the match I was inclined towards playing the spinner. I had said as much to the assembled media men the previous afternoon, on the terrace outside Headingley's modern, two-storey pavilion – and, despite Ted's views on keeping our strategy confidential, it was not an intentionally misleading remark. John is a high-class bowler, capable of playing either an attacking or a defensive role, and I felt we would be stronger for the variety he would provide.

If anything, it was the gloomy weather forecast on breakfast television which confused the issue. It spoke solemnly of rain and more rain in the days to come. Such weather would not exactly have been unusual during a Leeds Test and when I spoke with Ted at breakfast time he has begun to think along the lines of a game restricted to three and a half days. Doubtless influenced by the heavy cloud cover over our hotel, he had come around to

The shape of things to come? Graham Gooch
offering the benefit of his experience

the belief that our best route to victory within the possibly limited time available was by giving our strongest seam attack first use of the prevailing conditions. He was evidently not alone in this theory for when we gathered in the middle at Headingly – our brains trust of captain, management and senior players – there was a mounting mood in favour of omitting the slow bowler. I allowed myself to go along with it, but I was full of regrets even before the day was out.

With that much admitted, I still felt a shade let down by the bowlers who did play. I believed then, and still do, that we picked the best available set of quicker bowlers for the likely conditions at Headingley. They simply failed to do themselves justice, and when players so conspicuously underperform there is a limit to the powers of any captain.

At the squad selection meeting we had cast our minds back to 1985, when the swing bowling of Richard Ellison had been so influential in the last two Tests. We won both those matches by an innings while Ellison took a total of seventeen wickets. The Australians were so hapless against him that it seemed logical to nominate a bowler of similar type to do that same job. We settled on Phil Newport, who not only had a good recent record for his county, Worcestershire, but had also taken eleven wickets against the touring side no more than three weeks earlier. He seemed ideal – a strong young bowler who swings the ball consistently – and we were not to know he would endure a complete nightmare. Nervous at first, Newport was then not permitted to settle by the Australian batsmen. Worst of all, he never threatened to swing the ball, which is where all our best-laid plans foundered.

A more contentious selection, and one over which we agonised at length, was Phil DeFreitas ahead of Paul Jarvis. DeFreitas has often been thought a more effective bowler in one-day cricket, a theory supported by his record to date, and I gave more credence to that argument than to the one which claimed Jarvis should play because this was his home ground. Jarvis had, none the less, been bowling sharply and effectively for Yorkshire and he virtually came within a toss of a coin of selection. It is easy to wonder whether, late in the summer, this omission weighed on his mind when he sized up the offer to go to South Africa . . . but then, that is another story.

DeFreitas was, in any case, not our worst bowler on that fateful first day, though to say anyone bowled to potential would be stretching a point. It is never easy for a captain to keep his players bubbling when their hopes have been damaged so early and so severely, not to mention when some of them are acutely aware of just how badly they are performing. Mike Gatting would always do a good deal of clapping and shouting, but it is not my style to be so demonstrative and probably never will be. I concentrated on regular, quiet, encouraging chats with the suffering bowlers, advising them that if the ball was not moving around as much as we had hoped then at least we should aim to bowl maidens and apply pressure in that way. Sad to relate and harrowing to observe, we could not even do that with any facility. Newport was confused to the point of depression and even Neil Foster, on whose experience I had placed a good deal of reliance, was visibly and audibly unhappy about his bowling.

The day inevitably had an Australian hero, but he was a name and face unfamiliar to English audiences. At least, he was at the time. Come the end of the summer and all English supporters had seen more than they would have chosen of Mark Taylor. Most amateur pundits would not even have picked him. Australia had an established and apparently effective opening pair in Geoff Marsh and David Boon, very different in their batting styles but close off the field as well as on it and willing to devote hours to the understanding which is essential in batting partners. Australia arrived in England with the pre-set plan of breaking up that pairing to install Taylor, a left-hander, alongside Marsh, and they persisted with it despite Taylor's comparative lack of form in the lead-up to the Tests. When decisions such as this bear fruit they are hailed as a triumph of man-management; when they fail, it is blind faith and folly.

We had, ironically, dismissed both Marsh and Boon (who came in at number three) by soon after lunch. At 57 for 2, I was encouraged to believe that things might yet turn out for the best. But it was then that Border came in to play a curious yet crucial innings. It was curious for his unusual show of nerves. The crowd may have assumed that his instant shot-making was a sign of cavalier confidence but from the middle, where I stood, it looked very much like the opposite. He was hitting out almost randomly in search of that elusive confidence. Instead of settling in and then playing shots, as he would conventionally have done, he played shots and then settled in. It can work – I have successfully done it myself in similar circumstances – and although we might have had him more than once, it worked that day as Border made 66 in less than two hours.

Taylor finished the day on 96 not out and seemed far from fretful at having to sleep on the wait for his first Test century. He had played only two previous Tests, in the Australians' recent series against the West Indies, and although he did not make a score of substance in either of them he was run out twice in the second, so came to England as an unknown quantity. To be frank, he did not immediately impress. He started sketchily and might have been fortunate to survive the first session, but the longer he stayed the more solid he became. Our bowling gave him width to express himself outside off-stump and by the end of the day I had seen quite enough of the Taylor

RIGHT: Not a sight I had bargained for when putting Australia in to bat at Headingley . . . Mark Taylor greets his first century of the series

FAR RIGHT: It seems odd, now, to reflect that Steve Waugh began the Headingley Test still seeking his first century at this level

cover-drive. By the end of the series I was seeing it in my sleep as he completed an aggregate rivalled, in Ashes series, by no one except a man named Bradman who, I am reliably told, could also play a bit.

Bad turned to worse on the second day. Australia proceeded serenely to 580 for 6, with no sign of an end to the torture, and if we had all been grudgingly impressed by Taylor on day one, we were little short of stunned by Steve Waugh on day two. It seems odd, now, to reflect that Waugh began this game still seeking his first century in Test cricket. He had made good runs for Australia, and they always maintained faith in his class, but I had never imagined he had quite the potential to bat like this. He played quite superbly, in the style of a man who scores hundreds as of habit.

By late afternoon, weary and ever more frustrated, I had to resort to deep-set fields, offering Waugh singles to sacrifice the strike. It did not always work. Whenever our bowlers dropped short or strayed in their line, as they did regrettably often, he crashed the ball to the square boundaries with enormous power. His timing off his legs was that of a player in rare touch, and his sublime command of the situation was such that I might have enjoyed watching him if I had not been on the receiving end of the assault. My perception of his innings was jaundiced by the state of the game – in our case, dire.

To any team which has been chasing leather so unprofitably for two days, it is the ultimate humiliation to encounter a tail-ender, an alleged 'rabbit', who proceeds to treat your bowling with offensive disdain. This now happended to our footsore attack as Merv Hughes, who had been nobody's idea of a Test batsman when last we saw him in Australia two winters earlier, laid about him to such spectacular effect that he made an unbeaten 63 out of the 139 runs Australia added in the final session.

All that was left to us, when finally we were allowed to pick up a bat on the Saturday morning, was to try to occupy the crease as long as possible. The follow-on figure was a remote but essential landmark; by the end of Saturday's play we were still 118 short, with four good wickets gone.

I had to face the press and I did not look forward to it. Saturday night press conferences had become established during home series but, while I could appreciate the public relations value behind them, I felt that this often put one or other captain in an invidious position. This was a view that was to harden in my mind as the summer progressed, with varying results, but on this first weekend of the series I got through the ordeal unscathed.

The captains who led England against the West Indies in 1988 (and there were quite a few of them) reckoned that the first question at the mid-match conference was invariably: 'Can we save it, Mike/John/Chris/Graham?' Now

I know how they felt. The question was duly, and I suppose justifiably, put to me and, naturally enough, my answer was that we could and should save it. It is a fact of life that the man in the hot seat at such stressful times will not give voice to the fears niggling away at his subconscious mind. Rather, he will say what he must in order to give the right public impression of confidence in his team. You have to back your own players as a captain, whatever your private misgivings, and although I honestly felt that we *ought* to avoid the follow-on, my faith in events taking the prescribed course had already been badly shaken.

As it transpired, we cleared the first hurdle, though not with very much to spare. Allan Lamb, whose persistent injuries later in the series were such a handicap to us, carried us past the follow-on mark with a typically pugnacious century, and although a day and a half remained I felt protected, if not immune from defeat. I did not think Australia had sufficient time to press home their advantage. I was wrong.

Border declared for the second time in the game (a very unusual route to winning a modern Test match) and we were left with a little more than two sessions to survive. It should not have taxed us greatly on a pitch far from devilish, despite its tendency to low bounce, but somehow we managed to snatch defeat from the jaws of safety.

If the batting was the final calamity, the bowlers again could not escape censure. With the Australians seeking quick runs for a possible declaration, we obliged them with bowling that verged on the philanthropic. On the final morning we conceded 72 runs in 10 dreadful overs littered with wides and no-balls. It was simply unprofessional and it allowed the Australians to begin the decisive phase of the game with their tails up, which in turn made life tougher for our batsmen.

With that said, it remains a mystery to me how we lost. Border, I felt, had almost delayed his declaration too long, which was obviously to our advantage. I didn't blame him. If it had been later in the series he would probably have left us fewer runs to make and more time to make them, but no shrewd captain – and 'AB' is very definitely shrewd – will ever gamble with the first Test of six. So he set us to score 402 in 83 overs and, of course, it was impossible. We could not even waste time contemplating victory and yet, at lunch, we had raced along to 66 for 1 and were going too well for our own good. Was victory really impossible? We had to keep all such thoughts concealed, in the certain knowledge that two quick wickets could put a very different complexion on the game. And that is precisely what happened. Barnett and Lamb were out directly after lunch. An hour later, Robin Smith and I followed in similar succession. We were on the slide.

My own dismissal caused some apoplexy among the media. I was out to a

wicket-keeping catch down the leg side for the second time in the match, and there was some talk on the radio and some words in certain newspapers to the effect that I had been the victim of a preconceived plan. Frankly, I thought the suggestion facetious. Sure, there are better ways of playing a leg-glance than I showed here, but to suggest that any international bowler sets out to dismiss a Test batsman by bowling outside his leg stump seemed utter nonsense, especially as the first of these dismissals came from a genuinely errant and very slow looosener from Lawson!

The match-winner that afternoon was Terry Alderman. If Australia were to bowl us out, it was always likely to be so. Alderman had long experience

ABOVE: *Alderman, man of the match, relaxes at the end of it all . . .*

. . . while his team-mates celebrate in typical Australian fashion

of English conditions and, more important, the skill to exploit them. Throughout the series he was a thorn in our side, moving the ball around a little off the seam but essentially succeeding by bowling consistently straight, something our own bowlers signally failed to emulate. Although, at Headingley, we batted very badly on that last afternoon, I considered we had lost the game over the first two days, when our bowling fell a long way below the required Test-match standard.

It hardly needs saying that our dressing room, afterwards, had all the atmosphere of a morgue, not improved by the rowdy celebrations getting into full swing just along the corridor. There was little of value to be said to our players at such a moment; they knew where they had gone wrong. But I had to talk to the press, gathered like hawks in the downstairs dining room, and I dare say I looked quite emotional as I said my piece. I was not on the point of bursting into tears – no one game is that important – but I did have a strong desire to express my precise feeling without being sidetracked. I wanted to say that we had bowled badly, that we had been outplayed in every aspect of the game. I did not want to dwell on the injuries which had deprived us of Botham, Dilley and, at very short notice, Gatting. I wanted to be precise in my level of dismay without giving way to either false excuses or false condemnation . . . and then, I had to tell them about my shoulder.

The fact that I had a chronic shoulder condition was not exactly news. Anyone watching me field would know: I could not throw properly. But it had sharply deteriorated over the course of that game and was thoroughly painful in the field. I did not consider it had hampered my batting and I made it plain that this was no sort of excuse, but I had taken advice and was now going to submit to some exploratory surgery. I was aware that the timing was bad. Lord's, and the next Test, was only nine days distant, and after what had just taken place, this was no time to be risking missing a match. But the specialist had assured me I would be recovered in ample time, and, modern keyhole surgery being what it is, I had no real doubts. As it turned out, the shoulder would never feel better during the entire summer than it did at Lord's.

CHAPTER FOUR

The Pressure Mounts

The most memorably satisfying innings are those which achieve a purpose – either saving or winning a match. A century scored in vain never quite means so much, even one attained under intense pressure. This was the way of it for me in the Second Test at Lord's. I scored 57 in the first innings and 106 in the second, but Australia still won convincingly and by the end of the game the tabloid press had begun calling for my head as captain.

If I considered this unfair I still had to admit that a proportion of the pressure upon me was self-inflicted. My notorious walk-out from the Saturday night press conference, filmed live and beamed to the nation on the evening news programmes, was a complete misjudgement, an instinctive reaction to tension which I regretted almost as soon as it was done. The inevitable inference drawn by the media was that I had lost control of the situation only midway through the second game of the series. It did not look good, I had to confess, and it was for that reason that I have seldom needed a century more than I did on the Monday; and I have seldom been more nervous about an innings.

I had gone into the game in good spirits. Headingley, I had convinced myself, had simply been an aberration and we could not play as badly again. Moreover, the surgeon had kept his promise, restoring some mobility to my shoulder without prejudicing my fitness for the game. There was inevitably some gloomy speculation in the press over my prospects of recovery, but it was never really an issue. The brief confinement, away from the telephone and the relentless public attention, may actually have done some good, helping to concentrate my mind and recover the optimism which had been so shockingly mislaid at Headingley.

I went into the operating theatre of a small London hospital at 10 a.m. on the Saturday and I was discharged twenty-four hours later. Leicestershire were playing a Refuge Assurance League match against Essex at Chelmsford, and I was able to motor over there in style, thanks to a thoughtful gesture from the chairman. Ted knows my love of smart cars and offered me the use of his Porsche for a few days.

Lacking any competitive cricket since the last Test, I reported to Lord's on the Tuesday, a day ahead of the rest of the team, for an extra practice. The shoulder felt fine. The surgeon had done enough to alleviate the immediate problem with the help of a needle and he had clearly hit the right spot. I knew it would need more attention at some future date but I was happy for that to wait until the season was over and glad that I had taken the remedial action I had.

There was good news and bad on the team front. Dilley was fit again and would naturally play, but Lamb had injured a finger and, although we delayed a decision until the morning of the match, he never looked like making it. This gave us no option but to include Gatting, which was a form risk. We picked him on reputation alone as he had not played since his hand injury when we selected the side. We did wonder what we would do if he made 0 and 1 against Surrey over the weekend – and, sure enough, he did. I just hoped his experience would see him through. We needed him at his best.

Three of the seam bowlers who had failed at Headingley had been replaced, and this time there was no question of Emburey being omitted. Gus Fraser, Middlesex's strong young seamer, joined the squad, and although he was the likeliest twelfth man I told him on the Wednesday that he had not been included just to make up the numbers. I wanted him to savour the possibility of playing. I also wanted him to hear it from me if he was left out. I still have a vivid recall of Robin Jackman arriving for the Lord's Centenary Test to find that he had been booked into the hotel for only two nights. You know where you stand when that happens.

I won the toss again and this time had no hesitation in batting. It would be wrong to claim I put Headingley right out of my mind when making the decision. I could not totally ignore the memory. But I would have done the same even if this had been the First Test. It looked a good pitch, and so it was.

There is invariably some movement off the pitch in the first session at Lord's and, as ever, we had to apply ourselves to negotiate this crucial passage without heavy casualties. Instead, we lost three wickets for 58. The third, and saddest, of them was 'Gatt', out for 0 to realise our worst fears.

The afternoon session was extraordinary because, despite being in some trouble, we scored 124 runs at almost five an over. We also lost four more wickets – among them Gooch for a solid 60 and myself for a pretty rapid 57. There was a spell, in mid-afternoon, when Robin Smith and I seemed to do little else but hit boundaries as we put on almost 50 in half a dozen overs.

42

There are some excellent traditions about the Lord's Test. One of them is meeting the Queen, an honour for any sportsman

Mike Gatting's selection was a gamble, as he had played very little cricket after injury. It failed – he was caught at short-leg for nought

TOP: *It is safe to say that I have felt and looked more relaxed than this, even at press conferences . . .*

. . . not that I stayed that long! As soon as I was out of the gates, I felt ten times better, and grabbed a taxi to the theatre and 'Anything Goes'

RIGHT: *The Australian slip cordon of (left to right) Taylor, Alderman and Border, soon had plenty to shout about once more*

This probably seemed a shade cavalier in the circumstances, but there were a lot of loose balls to be hit and we could see no profit in ignoring them. The annoying part was that, having established some sort of command over the bowling, we both got ourselves out, and although Jack Russell showed what an improved batsman he is with an unbeaten 64, we were dismissed before the close for 286. I reckoned that to be about 150 below par, and once again the Australians made us pay for it.

Friday, however, belonged to us. It was one of those golden days unique to Lord's, when the ground is full, the cricket tense and the atmosphere buzzes with excitement – the sort of day that makes Test cricket what it is. From 151 for 1, with Taylor and Boon well set, Australia declined to 265 for 6. We were right back in the game, and the last thing I said to the lads in the dressing room that evening was that we must work twice as hard the following day to make sure it did not slip away from us again.

Rather than slip, it clattered deafeningly away from us. Waugh, who looks a majestic player right now, made his second big, undefeated hundred and the last four wickets doubled the score with Geoff Lawson, batting at number ten, making 74. Trailing by an intimidating 242, we had a nasty session to bat through and made a hash of it. Gooch was out third ball, Barnett and Broad quickly followed and it was left to Gatting and Gower, who have seen their share of England crises down the years, to avert total surrender.

It had been a wretched day, one which began so full of promise but turned mockingly sour. Defeat confronted us again and I dreaded the press conference. I knew there was plenty to defend but I badly wanted to get away from the claustrophobia of the situation and think things through alone. There was, however, no getting away from the obligation to attend and I reacted in the worst imaginable way. My fuse, which is shorter than most people seem to believe, blew in quite spectacular style.

I was terribly tense when I walked into the marquee at the back of the pavilion, which had been rapidly transformed from tea-tent to conference room. Immediately, I sensed a hostile, unforgiving atmosphere. The media had plainly been unimpressed – rightly so – but it appeared I was in for a serious interrogation. I tried to be light, flippantly suggesting that the best plan might be for the assembled scribes to refer to the notes they had taken in similar circumstances at Headingley. It was a mistake. Because of my tension it sounded horribly wrong and I knew it as soon as the words were out.

The best way to reply – a hundred at Lord's against Australia made even more satisfying

A couple of the former players representing newspapers began to press me about using my bowlers at the wrong ends. This was something I had not anticipated. They made a big issue of why Neil Foster operated from the Pavilion End when, on Friday, he had been more effective from the Nursery. The fact was that I had offered him the chance to change ends after five overs in the morning but he had opted to stay as he was. I never managed to convey this because, by now, the journalists' expressions seemed as intimidating as the ranks of TV cameras facing me. I felt, rightly or wrongly, that it no longer mattered what I said because it would be misinterpreted anyway. Something had to go, and it was me!

My exit was not very dignified. Nor did it help that I offered the excuse of having to go to the theatre, especially as the show was 'Anything Goes' by that well-known cricketer, Tim Rice. The press naturally made capital out of that! But I was temporarily out of control. I snapped. Yet, no sooner was I through the tent flap and heading for the Grace Gates than I felt fine. I knew I had messed things up in a big way and I was instantly resigned to the repercussions, but I walked into St John's Wood Road with a smile on my face.

The fuse had been replaced.

Those who mistake me for a totally placid character were doubtless amazed by all this, but those who know me better will have seen my temper flare before. It had happened once, earlier in the summer, when BBC radio wanted to record an interview with me before a Sunday League game at Grace Road. It was being conducted by Charles Colville in the London studio and I objected to his line of questioning, which was basically getting at the selection of Ian Botham being apparently on reputation rather than form. When he persisted and rejected my support for Ian, I decided that the interview was becoming more suitable for Prime Minister's 'Question Time' than 'Sport on Two' and left. Fortunately, as this was a taped interview, I was able to collect my thoughts and return to the box later, to complete it in more amicable fashion.

It is not that I was ever unaware that media interest is an integral part of the England captaincy. I appreciated the need for it, and there have been times when I have actively enjoyed it. I certainly started the season full of good intentions as to the way I wanted things to happen. But on that fateful

LEFT: *Waugh celebrates victory at Lord's. Two more unbeaten scores there meant that he ended this match with 350 runs in the series, without once being out*

ABOVE: *It's a forced smile from me and a barely restrained smirk from him. The faces tell the story at the presentation ceremony at Lord's*

Saturday evening I handled things so badly because the pressure had got to me, and I knew that the summer was going to be full of tension from that moment on.

All the unwelcome publicity accorded to my walkout had its inevitable knee-jerk effect within the Board. Ted obviously had to involve himself and when the telephone in my hotel room rang on Sunday morning I was not remotely surprised to hear the chairman on the line. Nor did I offer any defence other than the authentic one, which was simply that such an interrogation, at the end of such a fraught day, would have taxed the patience of a saint. I realised, of course, that this was not good enough and Ted told me he would be issuing a statement to the media saying I had been reminded of my obligations. It was widely translated as a slap on the wrist, a reprimand. Fair enough. Ted, however, was sufficiently concerned about my state of mind to invite me down to his golf club, Sunningdale, for Sunday lunch. By then I had already made alternative plans to go to Hurlingham to watch the pre-Wimbledon get-together and some gentle, charity cricket in a properly carnival and relaxed atmosphere, a stark contrast to the press tent of the night before, but it was another nice touch from the chairman and I was grateful for his support.

Back at the cricket the following morning, my nerves were playing up in uncharacteristic style and I don't suppose I was at my cheeriest in the dressing room. It is one thing to want to do well when you go out to bat; it is quite another to need success as I did that morning. I did not even dare contemplate the headlines if I had been out early and we had lost by an innings with a day to spare. Fortunately, it did not happen. I scored the century I was after, and if it was far from being my most fluent, the relief was every bit as sweet. With Robin Smith, who was fast becoming an exciting new fixture in the team, adding a brave 96 we were at least able to set Australia a target. On Tuesday we even took four of their wickets. The result was made to look respectable if not acceptable, and I ended the game in better spirits, apologised to the press for Saturday's shambles and then took my worries off up the motorway system to Shropshire for a NatWest Trophy game, obliged to transfer my thoughts from a struggling Test side to my struggling county side.

A week later we were back on the international roundabout but still finding it just as hard to keep our balance. In fact, in the days prior to the Third Cornhill Test at Edgbaston I seriously began to wonder if fate was trying to do us a favour by cramming all our misfortune into as short a time as possible; soon, I wanted to convince myself, the clouds would miraculously clear from above our team and luck would turn with a vengeance.

I had to cheer myself up with the thought that nothing more could

Merv Hughes ends up on his backside after a Botham drive

possibly go wrong, because so much already had. The squad selected for the game began to disintegrate almost as soon as it was announced. Lamb and Smith, both crucial to our hopes of making a score to put pressure on the Australians, withdrew with injuries; then we lost Neil Foster, still arguably our best seam bowler. All this was occurring while I was marooned at Hinckley, playing a three-day game. Anyone who has ever been there will realise that Hinkley is not the ideal spot from which to communicate with fellow selectors over important decisions, and when Ted finally got through on the pavilion phone, it was the final session of our game and not a moment, I thought, to make a snap judgement.

Ted brought me up to date and gave me a short-list of three from which one batting replacement was to be summoned. I asked for a few hours' grace. I did not want to be rushed, but I also thought it was a principle worth establishing. I made a few tactical phone calls and studied some relevant figures before phoning the chairman with my view that it should be Tim Curtis.

Subconsciously settling for the team with which we were left, and consoling myself that things could be worse, I soon discovered that they were. When we arrived at Edgbaston on the Wednesday afternoon for the usual practice session, Mike Gatting was concerned about his mother-in-law, who had been unwell when he set off. Borrowing a mobile phone, he put in a routine call home and was told that she had died during his journey north. There is nothing useful one can say to a guy who has just received that sort of

news, and there was obviously no way he was going to stay another minute in Birmingham. Our sympathies were very much with him as he left to return to London.

In pragmatic terms, however, this meant that we needed to summon yet another replacement at very short notice. Resisting any temptation to take a complete flier with an outright newcomer, we called up Chris Tavaré, whose move from Kent to Somerset seemed to have given his career new motivation (something which was to prey on my mind as I deliberated my own future much later in the year). 'Tav' is a fine player but it was five years since his last Test, and on receiving the call to join the squad, he got into an immediate flap about his England kit, which had apparently been consigned to mothballs.

The un-English scene at Edgbaston on Friday night after a spectacular tropical storm had left the ground, and the surrounding roads, under water

BELOW: *Dean Jones' century carried the Australians out of reach after we had taken three wickets cheaply*

RIGHT: *Ian Botham, back in the England side after further injury problems, batted doggedly for 2½ hours before being bowled by Merv Hughes*

Amid all the enforced changes we at last had Ian Botham back in the fold. Having earned his place in the one-day squad, and proved his recovery from back surgery, I know how dismayed he was when a broken cheekbone, suffered in a county game, discounted him from the first two Tests. He may not have demanded a recall through weight of runs or wickets but Australia, I am sure, would far rather he was not playing. Some things never change, and Ian's fighting spirit is one of them. At practice, quite unbowed by all the calamities which had befallen our plans, he was bursting with enthusiasm and displaying that brash confidence which cannot fail to be infectious.

By the second evening of the game I was cursing the first bad weather in months, which appeared to have compromised our best position of the series. By the fourth evening, I was silently grateful for the suddenly fickle

BELOW: *Border had just passed 8000 Test runs when he was bowled round his legs by Emburey. Australia's captain looks suitably perplexed*

English weather. Australia had been 298 for 7 before, for the third consecutive Test, we allowed their tail-enders far too much scope. They totalled 424 and although we could not even begin our reply until just before lunch on Monday, at 75 for 5 we were making up for lost time in alarming fashion.

I lost the toss for a change, but although for preference I would have batted first, I still had to be happy with the way the first day went. I seemed to get the bowlers on at the right times, even from the right ends, and for the first time in three games the Australian batsmen never got away from us.

In Foster's absence, Gus Fraser made the debut he had missed out on at Lord's, and impressed in every way. He is an old-fashioned English seam bowler, the sort to win the approval of that demanding old-timer, Alec Bedser. Line and length are his stock-in-trade and his disgust at wasting a ball is a good sign. Despite his relative youth he also fitted into the dressing-room atmosphere. He has no hang-ups, because he has grown so accustomed to the Middlesex side in which accomplished cricketers and strong characters vastly outnumber youngsters. In that sort of environment you grow up fast or suffer, and Gus has plainly learned. He took the mickey out of John Emburey quite mercilessly.

The abiding memory of that first day, however, was the storm which broke, shortly before the scheduled close. It was spectacular, almost tropical in its intensity, and as I stared out of the dressing room window across the ground, the press box on the far side disappeared into the dramatic murk. At least, I swore that it did – others felt this was just wishful thinking. Getting from pavilion to car was treacherous enough; steering it through a foot and a half of water might have been more interesting but for the Audi's four-wheel drive.

The time lost on the Friday and Saturday meant that a positive result was highly improbable, but the longer Dean Jones batted the less frustrated I could afford to feel. Jones is an archetypal Australian, with a cockiness in the middle which can be intensely irritating, but there is no doubt he can play. Not the least impressive feature of his 157 was that he made them at a very good pace, while most other batsmen were struggling. He never dawdles and he was last out on Monday morning after shepherding the tail-enders through that vital and, for us, miserably disappointing passage.

Not for the first occasion, they got us in at a difficult time. It sounds suspiciously like an excuse but the fact remains that for a period either side of lunch the ball began to move around. Alderman and Lawson were not slow to exploit it. Gooch went cheaply, lbw again and now seriously concerned about his form, and I made only 8. At 75 for 5 the follow-on target looked a million miles away, but Botham batted sensibly for 46 until unaccountably missing a straight ball, while Jack Russell was again a revelation.

Jack had been in awful trouble against the short ball, especially from Merv Hughes, during the First Test at Headingley, but his solution was to work extra hard in the nets, concentrating on the specifics of countering another such assault. He showed immediate benefit at Lord's and maintained the improvement here. He is such a high-class wicket-keeper that we should not demand runs from him, but if he makes them with any regularity it is a welcome bonus to the team. He is a quiet, steady character

Waugh is out for the first time in the series –
bowled by Fraser for an aggregate 393

but a live-wire in the field, always encouraging the bowlers and keeping his captain informed as to how the ball or the pitch is behaving – a real acquisition to the England side.

Come Tuesday morning and we were confronted with a simple equation. At 185 for 7 we required another 40 runs to avoid being asked to follow on. Before play resumed, Micky and I called the dressing room to order and had a few well-chosen words with the boys. We spoke at length about how much was at stake and tried to inject them with confidence. It worked to the extent that we saved the follow-on, and with it the game, but it was an agonising ninety minutes in coming.

We lost one wicket immediately – and to a wholly unnecessary run-out at that. Then the ninth wicket went down with 10 runs still needed. There was a great deal of anxious pacing inside the dressing room and Micky and I reached an understanding, based unashamedly on superstition. I had been watching the game on TV but had gone out to the balcony when the run-out occurred; Micky had then left his balcony post and come inside just as Emburey was out. We decided to stick rigidly to our positions: the captain inside, the manager outside. The relief, when Jarvis hit the all-important four, was indescribable.

More than four hours of the game remained when Australia went in again, and with a comfortable cushion of 182 runs, I suspected they would seek a quick declaration if only to press home a psychological advantage. I was immensely grateful when they elected to bat out the day instead. The way things had been going, I was perfectly content out there in the field, although, as the game ended, my dearest wish remained that we should put them under the same kind of batting pressure we had faced in each game to date.

CHAPTER FIVE

Dark Days and Drama in Manchester

Old Trafford was the nadir of my season as captain. Never have I known a match in which my emotions have been laid so bare. Resignation became an issue during the game; so, too, did my relationships with the media and the England committee. The Ashes were irretrievably lost at Old Trafford. So, amidst all this grief, it is the greatest of ironies that I actually ended the game more secure in the job than I had been a week earlier, and more enthusiastic about the remainder of the summer.

The catalyst for this dramatic change of situation was South Africa. The official confirmation of prolonged rumours about another English tour, inevitably labelled a 'rebel tour', meant that attention was deflected from the captaincy, and the inclusion in the South African party of Mike Gatting meant that the popular alternative as captain had cancelled his nomination.

If this news undeniably altered my outlook in the immediate future, I cannot pretend that it was all good news. No one as involved in English cricket as I have been likes to see so many leading players abandoning their Test careers at the stroke of a pen. It invoked another inevitable period of team rebuilding, and while I did not know at the time that my part in this was destined to be strictly short-term, I was tempted to guess from certain information which in my blackest moments I thought was being kept from me by the England committee. One item was their own, detailed file on which players were wanted for the tour to South Africa; the other, less grave but equally significant, was the process of establishing players' availability for the winter tours.

I received a letter from the Board shortly before the Old Trafford game began. It was a stereotype form asking whether I would care to be considered for one or both of the scheduled winter trips. No problem there – I put the relevant ticks against everything and sent it back to Lord's. Apparently thirty such letters went out to players chosen by the selectors as likely candidates – except that I was one of those selectors, and I had

not been consulted over who should be 'carded'. It occurred to me at the time that it could not be right to leave the captain out of such discussions, and it niggled at me periodically thereafter. Were they trying to tell me something? Or was it simply a matter of routine, a case of not wishing to add to the list of problems?

I appeased myself with the thought that my role in Test team selection still seemed undiminished, whatever the private reservations of my fellow committee members. Certainly, the newspaper headlines I often saw, criticising 'Dexter's choice', were misleading. As he had pledged when the summer began, Ted, while having thoughts of his own and airing them, did not impose his chairman's power overmuch. Micky always came to selection meetings armed with files and his input was, as a consequence, very detailed, but if I expressed a strong opinion about a certain player I was seldom overruled. Ted's view, and one which Micky did not dispute, was that the captain must, within reason, have players in whom he has confidence.

This general policy was maintained when the team for Old Trafford was selected. As ever when England are fairing badly, there was a knee-jerk reaction from sections of the press amounting to a demand to sack all the current players, no matter what their accomplishments, and start again with young and untried stock. There was, of course, a more realistic argument for introducing deserving youngsters on a selective basis, but even this, I felt, was ill-conceived. My conviction remained that our best chance of getting back into the series from a parlous position of two down with three to

FAR LEFT: Ted shows me the list of players who are now confirmed for a South African tour. Any thoughts of resignation must now be redundant

LEFT: One of our successes of the summer was Robin Smith. He made 143 at Old Trafford and I quickly came to enjoy batting with him. We now share a county dressing-room, too

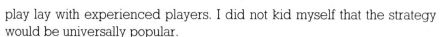

play lay with experienced players. I did not kid myself that the strategy would be universally popular.

There were side-issues to bother and distract me as the game approached, not least the continuing poor form of my county, Leicestershire. There is undoubted truth in the theory that county fortunes, good or bad, are carried with you into Test cricket. Leicestershire were having another very disappointing year for a side of considerable talent, and however capably I compartmentalised my life it would undoubtedly have helped with England if things were going better at Leicester. The reverse might equally have been true in the sense that I might have had more energy to help cope with the county's problems. Between the Third and Fourth Tests, Leicester's stock fell to its lowest level when we were not just beaten, but humiliated by Sussex in the NatWest Trophy, our last chance to give the season some meaning.

On the Sunday before the Manchester game, one tabloid newspaper allowed its imagination to run riot with a story claiming I would quit the captaincy if we lost. Their writer had phoned me the previous morning, in the Taunton hotel where Leicestershire were staying. I came out of the shower to answer the call and I was anxious to get back in it, so I gave what I felt was a simple, non-committal response to what was transparently a loaded question. I told him that if we were to lose the next game, and with it the series, then naturally I would have to *consider* my position. From the way the story was portrayed, however, five million readers were left with the impression that I was on the point of resigning. It certainly didn't help!

Whatever my personal outlook however, this was a crisis match. Lose it, and the Ashes were gone. Draw, and we would be left with the mountainous task of winning the last two to salvage something. It was built up, not without justification, as the match England had to win, and I was uncomfortably aware of the potential reaction if we were to fail.

Part of the sporting press had by this time adopted an openly belligerent stance. Hardly a day passed without sackings or resignations being demanded in print. One of the tackier tabloids had amused itself, if not its readers, with insulting line-drawings of me, and other England players, wearing dunces' caps. I found it all pretty offensive and the entire subject of dealing with the media had begun to irk me more than I had expected. The line-up of travelling cricket writers had altered dramatically since my previous tenure as captain; in some cases, I suspected, so too had the motivation.

It was soon clear that I should brace myself for the explosion, because yet again we put ourselves under pressure by batting poorly. We made only 260, of which substantially more than half were scored by Robin Smith, who matured before our eyes in the course of a series which left so many other reputations in tatters. Robin may have suffered early in his career from extravagant expectations. His advance publicity, as allegedly the more talented of two brothers who have now both played for England, might easily have been counter-productive, giving him too much to live up to at an impressionable stage of his cricket education. When he came into the Hampshire side as a teenager it was soon evident that he had the flair and the power to be an exciting player, but he still had to learn to build an innings and to occupy the crease for long periods. This has taken him some time to master, but he is an incredibly determined character. In a summer without much to commend it, he and Jack Russell were already shining exceptions to the mood.

This time it was Geoff Lawson who bowled us out, which was at least a variation on the Alderman theme, if not an improvement. I managed 35 but it was not remotely enough to give us a negotiable score and, sadly, those of us who have been around at top level for years were plainly not having the expected impact on the series. Gatting was still out of the side, apparently recovering his form and spirits, but, as we were soon to learn, never to return. Lamb was injured again and, to my dismay, out for the remainder of the series. I missed him not just as a high-class player but as a good friend and a splendid, uplifting influence in the dressing room. He was enduring an amazing sequence of misfortunes for a guy who had sailed through most of his career with not so much as a muscle twinge to bother him. Gooch was still with us but making very few runs and fretting about it. As for Botham, he got himself out with as ambitious a slog as you could fear to see from a Test player whose score stood at nought. It was an awful moment and I have seldom seen him so downcast, though it must be added that Ian's concentration on the match was not exactly helped by various events off the field including death threats, which the Manchester police were certainly taking seriously.

The dressing room, in fact, was not a happy place. Everyone was understandably tense over the position of the series and the fact that we had not once done justice to our potential and put the opposition under any kind of pressure. I was doing my best to cheer players up on an individual basis, reassuring and encouraging them, but in two spells as England captain I do not think I had ever found it more difficult, which doubtless said something about my own state of mind.

The team atmosphere was not helped, indeed I would now go so far as to say it was directly damaged, by constant rumours about the South African tour, extending to certain newspapers speculating over who would be going. I had no idea, other than the knowledge that I had not even been

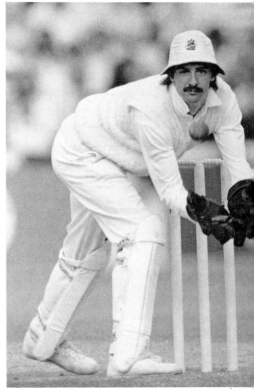

asked, but I was finding this continuous sub-plot irksome and distracting.

By Saturday evening Australia were already 181 ahead and still batting. Of their top six only David Boon had missed out, and although nobody made a hundred, Waugh scored 92 and the remarkable, metronomic Taylor made 85. It was a long and unrewarding slog in the field for us as Australia cashed in on what was a perfectly good pitch. The rest day beckoned like a haven, but I was not even permitted to enjoy that in peace.

I missed the Saturday night press conference, but not through my own in-itiative. Micky had been discussing the situation with officials of the Board and when I came off the field, weary and disconsolate, he told me not to bother attending as it would achieve nothing. I was grateful and relieved at the time, as it was not likely to be a convivial gathering, but in hindsight I realise they had been worried that I might be in a mood spontaneously to annouce my resignation if the questioning had not been to my liking. I am perfectly confident that this would not have happened, because I didn't feel like resigning then. By Sunday morning, I did.

Resignation began to seem an attractive option when I was apprised of a

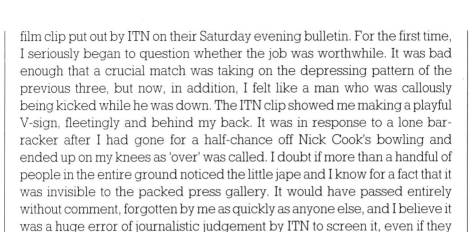

film clip put out by ITN on their Saturday evening bulletin. For the first time, I seriously began to question whether the job was worthwhile. It was bad enough that a crucial match was taking on the depressing pattern of the previous three, but now, in addition, I felt like a man who was callously being kicked while he was down. The ITN clip showed me making a playful V-sign, fleetingly and behind my back. It was in response to a lone bar-racker after I had gone for a half-chance off Nick Cook's bowling and ended up on my knees as 'over' was called. I doubt if more than a handful of people in the entire ground noticed the little jape and I know for a fact that it was invisible to the packed press gallery. It would have passed entirely without comment, forgotten by me as quickly as anyone else, and I believe it was a huge error of journalistic judgement by ITN to screen it, even if they did think they were seeing the funny side.

What followed was ten times worse. Sections of the press over-reacted, predictably but laughably, and early on Sunday morning my lie-in was interrupted by a phone call from the chairman. Ted told me he felt he needed to issue a statement of some sort to defuse the situation. I replied that, in my view, to say anything would be to give the thing a credence it did not deserve. It would also, inevitably, be interpreted as a second rep-rimand for the errant captain. My arguments failed. Ted insisted that some-thing was necessary, and for the first and only time during that summer, I felt he was taking sides against me. It depressed me enormously and I spent the rest of the day fuming, my mind in turmoil over the value of perse-vering in a job which was bringing me little but hassle.

In my black mood, I could see no reason for persisting in my efforts to maintain a relationship with the media. There was, it seemed, nothing left to preserve. I could not believe there was any justification for the witch-hunt and the thought certainly crossed my mind that, if they wanted me out of the job so badly, I might just give them satisfaction.

It took me a long time that day to get back to something approaching nor-mal. Lunch in the wilds of Cheshire was suitably subdued, and it was only during the afternoon, relaxing with friends in Hale, that the clouds started to lift. Seldom had I felt such little enthusiasm for the following day's Test match.

Thankfully, the depression did not last. Twenty-four hours later my personal inclinations were far less defeatist, even though, out on the field, we were heading inexorably for another beating. Bob Willis, who went down a similar rocky road as captain, took me for a bottle in a Hale wine bar on Monday evening and his company was stimulating. He kept asking me what I wanted out of life – testing me out, if you like – and I came round to the view that I should not resign simply to keep the tabloid scribes happy. Call it

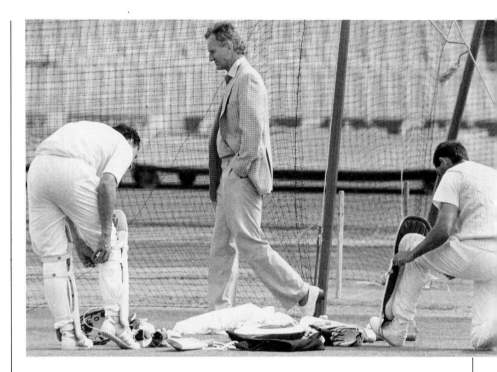

bloody-minded if you like, but I regarded it as being rational, too. I had been given a job for the summer and, now that I had emerged from the dark tunnel that was Sunday, I still had the desire to see it through.

Come Tuesday and all doubt had gone. Everything had changed. We lost the Fourth Test by nine wickets, and we had lost the Ashes, at 0 – 3 with two to play, but there was no longer any possible question of resignation. To walk out on the job on the very day that the game was rocked by final authentification of all the South African rumours would have been unthinkable.

Ted, in any case, again made it clear that he wanted me to carry on. We stood together on the ground for about twenty minutes before play – a public summit, visible if not audible to all. Ted pre-empted anything I might have had in mind by repeating that I still had the full backing of his committee. After the other, sensational events of the morning, this was no more than a comforting endorsement of a decision already taken, but I appreciated his support none the less.

What I did not appreciate, and found more irritating as the full facts transpired, was that the England committee's advance knowledge of the South African situation has been kept from me. The Board's 'spies' had acquired a considerable amount of information about which players were committed to the project and all of it had been passed on to Ted and Micky. It would

FAR LEFT: *Ted Dexter had plenty on his mind prior to the Fourth Test at Old Trafford, not least the media speculation that his captain might consider resigning if we lost the game*

LEFT: *Even when things are not going your way it is nice to have a laugh with old mates (less of the old, please, I.T.B.)*

have been nice, not to mention useful in my job, if they had taken me into their confidence. I found it irksome to discover that I was working with two people through the summer on a small, apparently friendly committee without being in full possession of what was going on behind the scenes. I felt a little betrayed, a little offended. If they did not think they could trust me with the information, they did not know me at all.

People will doubtless find it hard to believe that the South African revelations took me quite so much by surprise, but the truth is that I knew nothing more than I had read in the papers. I had no idea that the tour party had been chosen and contracted, in a secret operation involving certain players well known to me and occupying several months, and it came as a particular jolt to learn that Mike Gatting had agreed to go. Somehow, despite all his problems and all his undisguised resentment over the way he believed the Board had mistreated him, I had thought it only a matter of time before we saw the old 'Gatt', large as life, back in the England fold. I had underestimated his sense of grievance as much as, I believe, he had underestimated the full, alarming implications of the venture.

The astounding inclusion, though, classically emphasising why I should have been kept abreast of developments, was that of Tim Robinson. Not because he was an improbable candidate for such a tour – he was not – but because the England selectors, with my full agreement, had recalled him to the team for this very game at Old Trafford. Naturally, if I had been apprised of his likely involvement, we would have looked to someone else – there was simply no future in including Robinson and I cannot imagine what went through his mind, both when he heard of his selection and, more poignantly, during the game itself. In the strange position of knowing it was to be his farewell Test, information denied to others, I can only assume he would have wished to do better.

Two other members of our Old Trafford team were named in the tour party, and when the news broke, they were affected in very different ways. For John Emburey, who had been to South Africa before and was an integral part of the group planning this trip, it worked well. He simply set out his stall to finish on a high note and succeeded, scoring 64 with the bat and then bowling well as we made Australia work a little for the 78 runs they needed. Neil Foster, however, was badly upset by the very public nature of the business and I am quite sure he would have given much to have been elsewhere when the team was announced. I understand why he chose to accept the South Africans' offer. His knee, long a cause for concern, was in such a state that he seemed very unlikely to play at the top level for much longer. A fat cheque for two short tours must have been a tempting pay-off. But, when we went out on the field for the final session of the game, and the final session of what had been a wholehearted England seam-bowling career, 'Fozzie' was crying. He tried manfully to bowl, and I tried to say the right things to him, but he was too emotional. I felt sorry for him, despite myself.

It seems crazy to relate that heavy defeat in a crucial game could lead to an improvement in team spirit, but that was quickly evident. No one expected us to save the series, which was a release. No one was looking over his shoulder for South African agents. It was out in the open and we could look to the future. I suddenly felt more enthusiastic.

CHAPTER SIX

Time to Step Down?

The Royal Hotel, in Nottingham's city centre, reverberates with night life. It boasts innumerable bars and restaurants, and most nights of the week revellers will come from miles around, dressed for a good time. A few years back, the previous chairman of selectors decreed that it was not a suitable place for the England team to stay. Fearing, rather fussily, that the players would be up to untold mischief in such a hotel, he elected to move us to a rural retreat as the base for Trent Bridge Tests. He nominated Rothley Court, near Leicester, and the result of that decision will for ever be ingrained on Mike Gatting's mind. It cost him the England captaincy and, indirectly, sent him into exile in South Africa.

One of many ways in which E.R. Dexter differed from P.B.H. May is that, in his view, city-centre hotels were preferable. And so, on Wednesday 9 August, trailing 3 – 0 but carrying the vague conviction that a fresh start was at hand, we checked in once more in the bustling lobby of the Royal.

Among the first things necessary, when we gathered in the dressing room at Trent Bridge, was a series of introductions. Although we had still not countenanced the 'sack the lot' theory and turned to a full platoon of callow youths, the loss of the series had undeniably shifted the goalposts a touch. The present was now not so important as the future. The outcome of this is that we selected two new caps, and if I hardly knew either of them at all, the same could be said for many of the others.

To some extent, I was presented with Devon Malcolm. It had sensibly been decided that nobody named in the party heading for South Africa would be considered, which extracted an alarming number of bowlers from the list of contenders – Dilley, Jarvis and, at the time, DeFreitas, in addition to Foster. We simply had to find at least one new quickie and both Ted and Micky had Malcolm on their lists. I knew little about him other than his reputation for being fast but wayward. I was in no position to argue.

Mike Atherton of Lancashire just got in ahead of Nasser Hussain. Again, I found it hard to separate these two on the limited evidence available. Both had been part of the Combined Universities side which performed so well in the Benson and Hedges Cup, and while Atherton, of Cambridge and Lancashire, had played more first-class cricket, Hussain, of Durham and Essex, seemed to have captured the imagination of the media. On the whole I felt we were justified, but when it came round to picking the winter tour teams the decision was reversed, Hussain going to the Caribbean and Atherton to Zimbabwe with the A team.

Two other changes were made, one enforced, one invited. Emburey's exit exposed what we already knew – that there is an acute shortage of quality slow bowling in the country – and although the choice of Eddie Hemmings, aged forty, was certain to be ridiculed by those urging us to give youth its chance, I was happy that we had picked the best from the alarmingly few spinners available.

Martyn Moxon's return was at the expense of Graham Gooch and led to some confusion. The truth is that Graham was certainly not dropped and neither did he positively exclude himself. What he did do, at the end of the Old Trafford Test, was to seek me out and express his worries. He felt he was not contributing and said that as he had been given plenty of chances, he would be happy to stand down from the next Test if we now felt it better to experiment. Whether, subsequently, he viewed our choice of Moxon as experimental or retrogressive I am not sure – the less complimentary opinion was certainly put by various newspapers – but in our position in the series it was easier than it might otherwise have been to accept his offer and look elsewhere.

The period between Tests had provided no sort of escape. Just when I needed it least, Leicestershire met the Australians in a three-day game at Grace Road. Mike Turner, Leicestershire's chief executive and very much my county boss, came on the phone almost as soon as I returned home from the Old Trafford debacle. 'If you are thinking of asking to drop out of the tourist game, don't,' was the gist of his message. I raised no objections, but I am sure Mike knew as well as I did that I would find it hard to motivate myself. There were so few incentives, given the current ambivalent attitude of most people involved towards matches between counties and the touring side. It was simply a question of making myself do it, knowing that if I happened to make a hundred I would have the nagging regret that I had not saved it for a Test, when it would really have mattered. This, I have to report, is one problem with which I did not have to cope.

What other spare time I had before Trent Bridge was eaten up by the trivial yet necessary jobs which so easily get neglected. The mail, for one thing. I had been getting a lot of letters, most of them gratifyingly supportive, and I tried to answer almost all of them. There were some business items which required my attention. And my social life needed reviving too. A couple of excellent restaurants in Leicester tended to get my business, primarily for their food but also because I was unlikely to be badgered there. Time away from the game is precious and, well-meaning though most people are, an interruption at dinner from someone eager to discuss Terry Alderman's late inswinger is not always welcome.

I tried, during this time, to avoid the cricket press. It never works. Inevitably, I got to see or hear most of what was written about me. It was impossible to ignore, and equally impossible not to take some of the comments personally and to feel hurt.

When Test time came round again, I put all such thoughts behind me, because I needed to be positive. Not just for my sake but for the rest of the players, some of them new and nervous. The captain is always expected to stand up and say his motivational piece on the eve of a game; often it is at the

Mid-afternoon on day one – and the Australian openers, undivided, enjoy a welcome drink . . .

71

team dinner, but on this occasion I addressed the troops in the dressing room at Trent Bridge. It went well enough. In fact, I was happy with my pre-game talks all through the summer, though there is irony in the fact that the best was undoubtedly given at Headingley, where it had mortifyingly little effect. There is only a certain amount of benefit that can be derived from a leader's words when the basic problem in his side is a lack of confidence. No captain can bat for his players; equally, at this level, he should not be telling them how to bat. It needs a turn in the wheel of fortune, an outstandingly good couple of days, to restore self-belief, and I would have given a great deal for that to happen at Trent Bridge.

I knew within twenty-four hours that it was a vain hope. We failed to take a

single wicket during a full first day's play. This, I was told, has not happened very often in the history of Test cricket and it is fair to say it was not the start we were looking for. But, although Taylor and Marsh had piled up more than 300, a phenomenal opening stand, I did not think we bowled badly. I was also impressed by the standard and spirit of the fielding and the fact that nobody allowed the events of the day to drag down team morale. Given the circumstances, it was a remarkably chirpy dressing room on Thursday evening.

My own sense of humour stood up better than had sometimes been the case. Towards the end of the afternoon, with both batsmen approaching 100 and our options running short, I waved the twelfth man, Greg Thomas, on to the field and, to his astonishment, asked him to nip round to the press box and ask the scribes what I should do next. Greg creased up with laughter. It was a light-hearted interlude which appealed to Ted, as I suspected it might, although Micky didn't seem to find it quite so amusing.

On the second day we achieved something of a breakthrough by dismissing Steve Waugh, whose series average was 242.50, for nought. The gloss was slightly taken off it by the fact that Australia's score, at the time, was 553 for 4. All we had left to aim for was the draw.

Marsh was out for 138 but the remorseless metronome that is Mark Taylor showed no such moderation. He amassed 219 in a little over nine hours. It was a monumental effort and elevated him to immortal company, as only Bradman had now totalled more runs for Australia in an Ashes series. It is easy to be lulled into underestimating Taylor, a far from flamboyant player, but he showed throughout the series that he had the technique, and the temperament, to sustain a high level of performance. He proved it, adding to his remarkable sequence of scores, in the Australians' subsequent home series with Pakistan.

Technical experts, and others purporting to be experts, made frequent unfavourable comparisons between the method of our own batsmen and that used by Taylor. To some extent, this was justified. Our techniques were made to look flawed, largely because it took most of the players more than one attempt to work out a serviceable method against the high-quality medium-paced swing bowling of Alderman. It might be said that this is a type of bowling encountered every day in county cricket, but this is to do Alderman no justice. In English conditions, there is only a handful of bowlers in his league.

A common criticism was that England batsmen were playing across their front pad against Alderman. This results either from getting forward too soon, and too far, or not getting there at all. It is a valid point, and many of us spent hours trying to correct the fault, but glibly to condemn anyone playing

RIGHT: Well may the chairman look grim. 0–4 is not what either of us had planned for the end of the Trent Bridge Test

BELOW: A sight that batsmen round the world will not find very pleasant, though Devon Malcolm's first day in Test cricket was memorable for the wrong reasons!

across the front pad makes Dean Jones a hopeless case. He hits off-stump balls through mid-wicket, entirely on the evidence of his eagle eyes. Strictly speaking, he is abusing the coaching manual, but it is mighty effective.

What concerned *me* about our batting, aside from any technical deficiency, was the acute shortage of confidence. The tentative way many of us played stemmed from the situations in which we continually found ourselves batting, for ever pursuing totals of 400 and upwards with crisis in the air. Our communal confidence was shattered early on, while the Australians never stopped growing in the stature which confidence feeds. Alderman, more than anyone, exploited this scenario to the full. To the outsider he must sometimes have resembled a puppeteer, England's best batters hanging on his strings. To us he became a torturer, never more so than on the Saturday morning of this Fifth Test.

Border declared early on that third day, once his total was past 600. Another psychological point scored against us. Soon, things were much worse – Moxon and Atherton gone, with only one run on the board. Alderman, yet again, had put them in complete control, but this time he was not to have things entirely his own way, as Robin Smith dealt out some rough treatment all round in a brilliant innings of 101. He refused to be subdued and played some quite staggering shots, yet his face was a picture of abject misery when he was out to a rash one against the first ball of a new spell from Alderman. He sat in the dressing room with head in hands like someone who has collected a 'pair' rather than a second century in successive Tests. The intensity of his ambition is really striking.

For all Smith's heroics, we were dismissed, soon after start of play on

So much for the idea of opening the second innings and trying to lead from the front – out first to a useful delivery from Lawson

Monday, for 255 and obliged to follow on 347 behind. By 4.15 p.m. we had been bowled out again for 167, losing our 'fresh start' match by the little matter of an innings and 180 runs. Mortifying is not the word.

I had decided in advance that I would open the innings myself when we followed on. There were a number of reasons for this. I had suspected for some time that Alderman was less effective and less comfortable against a left-hander; I wanted to withdraw Moxon from the firing line and felt he had the potential to stabilise a middle-order lacking Botham, who had damaged a hand; finally, and most persuasively, I wanted to give a positive lead.

It came to nothing. I was bowled in the second over, shouldering arms to

a ball from Lawson which, on its original line, would have missed off-stump comfortably. Somehow, no one seemed to give him much credit for an outstanding piece of bowling. Atherton made 47, an innings to give us some hope for the future, but eventually it was Merv Hughes, the pugilistic contrast to the steadiness of Alderman and Lawson, who took three wickets to finish us off. Within an hour of the game ending, the ground was awash beneath a storm of tropical proportions, appropriate for my gloomy mood.

I slipped quietly home down the A46 and really did not feel like venturing out of the house to face the world. There were no longer any thoughts of resignation in my head. I reasoned that I had been given a contract, albeit unwritten, for the summer, and that I would complete it. But I could not contemplate anything longer term. I was prepared for the fact that the final Test, at The Oval, was to be my last as captain. I was even looking forward to the release. Whatever the feelings of the other selectors, or the enduring strength of Ted's oft-repeated support, I had come to the conclusion that it was futile even to consider carrying on in the job. I longed to get back to some sort of normality. The job had not gone remotely in the way I had hoped. I felt a heavy sense of oppression and, as someone who places great

Not once in the series could we field the originally selected team but, at The Oval, the injury crisis reached new peaks. This was the eleven which finally represented us

store by the quality of life, this was not something I was prepared to tolerate indefinitely. Sad though it was, I believed I would be happier with the burden removed.

It was in this melancholy mood that I entered my last selection meeting. England selectors have convened in some odd places over the years, and remarkably seldom in the formal committee rooms most people imagine. Pubs, hotels, restaurants, dressing rooms and even motorway service areas have all been employed at some stage; the venue of this one was the kitchen of the Gower residence in Leicester. I was engaged in a Championship game against Surrey, so Ted and Micky drove up from London and we all adjourned to my place after close of play. There was something ironical about it, given the circumstances.

I did not give Ted or Micky any indication of how I felt about the future. That could wait. What was noticeable to me, though, was that my influence over selection had been weakened. It would be wrong to pretend it had ever been entirely at my discretion, but for these last two Tests there had been a conspicuous change. The policy, the framework of the team, was now being set by Ted and Micky before our meetings even began. I was now more following than leading in these discussions, part of which was undoubtedly due to my own diminishing confidence in the role.

My views had also begun to differ from those of the others in that I feared the consequences, and questioned the benefits, of throwing in too many youngsters. I was conditioned by having seen players, Gooch and Pringle among them, set back several years by being chosen too soon. I remained in favour of using players who had been around a little longer, had perhaps played a Test or two and turned in consistent performances at county level.

Policies, however, depend on fitness and this was one area in which luck shamefully neglected us, even at the very last. Not once in the series were we able to field the team originally selected, but the injury situation this particular week was so chaotic it might have been funny if it had not been so demoralising. Malcolm was the first to withdraw, with a back strain. DeFreitas, who by now had reversed his decision to go to South Africa, was summoned as replacement but then injured a hamstring. Fraser pulled out with knee trouble and Thomas, when approached to stand in, revealed that he was now committed to the South African squad as DeFreitas's replacement!

Micky then took over the recruitment of enough players to fill the team and, after a series of phone calls, came up with Pringle and the Kent quick bowler Alan Igglesden. I have no doubt it was a difficult day for the manager but it did not exactly help our fragile morale when, at the eve-of-match press conference, he remarked to the effect that Igglesden was the sixteenth choice fast bowler.

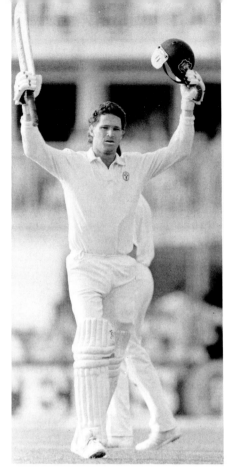

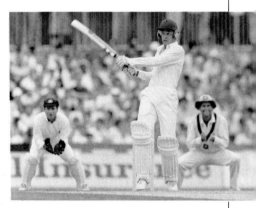

PREVIOUS PAGE: Australia once again batted us out of the game. Graham and I ponder the possibilities from slip – or is that a stifled yawn from my Essex friend?

LEFT: Confident as ever, and once more successful – Dean Jones and his second century of the series

BELOW: The Oval has been one of my more successful venues and I felt I played near my best during my first innings 79

Given our threadbare attack and the state of the series, it was a foregone conclusion that I would lose the toss on a belter of a pitch. In all the circumstances, then, we were doing remarkably well when Gladstone Small took his second wicket and Australia stood at 149 for 3. It was just another mirage. By the close of the first day, Jones and Border had put on 176 at a rattling pace, so already we were destined to bat under the customary pressure.

I was reminded, in a morbid way, of our 1982 – 3 tour to Australia. Robin Jackman, a very old friend, was on the trip and when we played against Victoria in Melbourne, I recall him being very scathing about a tall, flashy batsman in the opposition ranks: 'This bloke can't play. He'll never make a cricketer,' he said with that scornful air often adopted by senior players about young upstarts. The trouble is that such a comment is frequently the cue for the maligned individual to score thousands of runs at the highest level. It had happened again, because the player to whom 'Jackers' referred was Dean Jones, here making his second hundred of the season in less than two and a half hours. He averages more than 50 in Test cricket and, for all his arrogance at the crease and all his unorthodox ways, he really can play.

We did pretty well, the following day, to take the last seven Australian wickets for only 123, but any pride over that was banished when we were obliged to begin our reply in desperately bad light. Poor 'Goochie', recalled after just one match of voluntary exile, was out to the third ball of Alderman's first over. It was the fifth time he had been out lbw in the series and, although one or two of the decisions, this one included, were debatable, he plainly had a serious problem with Alderman's line.

Play was abandoned for the day soon after Graham's dismissal, and on Saturday rain drew a mercifully thick veil over proceedings soon after 3 p.m. Our greatly reorganised batting line-up had failed to improve our fortunes, and just after lunch we stood at 98 for 6 in reply to Australia's 468. Every time I consoled myself that things could not get worse, I was proved wrong.

We managed to avoid the follow-on, much against the odds, and I felt in pretty good nick in making 79. Border, though, refused to allow us off the hook and declared on the final afternoon to give us one last, familiar passage of pressure. For once, thank God, we survived it. We came out with a draw, confining the damage to 4 – 0, but we were very much second best again. The gulf between the two teams now seemed enormous, but I shall always be convinced that confidence and continuity were the key issues. Australia got through the series using only twelve players; we used twenty-nine, the majority of the changes enforced by injury.

The final press conference of the series passed off in relative peace. Even the most mischievous of the scribes seemed to have exhausted their bile, and Ted provoked the most reaction for saying he was not aware of having made any errors during the summer. As for me, I was quite pre-pared to admit to a few, if not as many as some would have me believe.

It had been a relentless series, impossible to enjoy because we never once got into a position to compete on equal terms. It all dated back to that very first day at Headingley, and if I regretted just one thing about the sum-mer, it was being persuaded to omit John Emburey and play that match without a slow bowler. By so doing, I gave credence to someone else's ideas and weakened my own authority. I will forever blame myself for that.

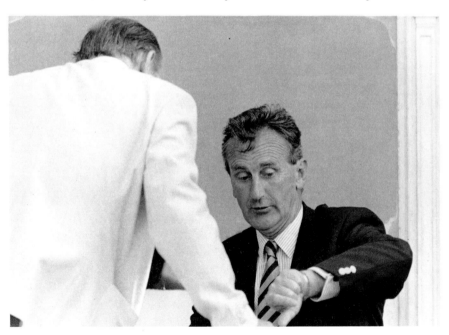

A complaint about over-rates? Slow batting?
Tardy service at lunch? The chairman
produces the timepiece evidence

CHAPTER SEVEN

Carrying the Can

Hindsight offers us all easy repentance, and looking back it is plain to me that the handover of the England captaincy was bungled by all concerned, not least myself. What I should have done, indeed what I had planned to do, was resign quietly and with dignity. Instead, personal pride and public sympathy combined to take me down a dead-end street. All of which made this next phase of my story more hurtful than was strictly necessary.

Over the weekend of the NatWest Trophy final I had arranged a few days' break in Portugal, combining a spot of promotional work with a very social game of cricket. It was something I had been wanting to do for ages and I looked forward to it. In my absence, however, the England committee was due to appoint the winter captains, so it was arranged that I would meet the chairman and team manager on Friday 1 September, to discuss our positions.

We met at Ted's house in Ealing, where the story had begun five months earlier. I arrived with strangely ambivalent feelings. I still thought it would be in my own best interests to stand down; the job had done me no good and, in my heart, I knew I was not in the right frame of mind to take a demoralised set of players to the Caribbean, where it is all too easy to be destroyed. But, pride having its say, I had no great wish to make any dramatic resignation speeches. I had also been influenced more than was good for me by the many people, some close to me and some total strangers, who had got in touch and urged me not to give up. Inevitably, this was flattering listening and so I entered the meeting with utterly confused intentions. I meant to tell them I had had enough, but I was also prepared to contemplate carrying on if they really wanted me to do so.

It soon became clear that my own views on the subject were worth precious little. Ted and Micky had been closeted together for an hour when I arrived, and they did not waste words. Ted ushered me to a chair and then told me that they had thoroughly discussed the situation and felt that they would like a change of direction.

The phrase 'change of direction' could mean only one thing so far as I was concerned, and although I could have jumped in at this point, revealed my case for giving up anyway and had the decision announced as a resignation, I didn't. I allowed them to lead me through the implications of what had been said, by which time it was plain I was 99 per cent certain to be sacked when the full committee convened the following Tuesday. I responded by telling them that I was content for them to release the decision in exactly the way it had just been explained to me – in other words, their conclusion that a change of direction was required.

I did not want them to camouflage the news with excuses about my shoulder condition. Someone would have seen through that easily enough and although I was by this time sufficiently aware of the discomfort to admit that it was affecting my technique and that I would be glad when the season was over and the surgery done, it remained a basically dishonest premise for sacking me.

Our gathering did not break up immediately, and certainly not with any overt bad feelings. In fact, we talked amicably about the future and I made the point to Micky that I believed the squad picked to tour the West Indies should have a training programme for the months prior to the trip. The scheme was acted upon, Micky doing the organising and receiving much credit. Ironical, that, as when I suggested it I had been under the firm impression that I would be one of those involved. At no stage of our chat did either Ted or Micky say anything to cast doubts in my mind. That shock was to come, one week later.

I set off for Portugal the following morning, still feeling sad that the job had gone so badly but unable to muster much grief about the loss of it. I knew, of course, that there had been ample scope for them to dismiss me after the events of the summer, and although the news was not yet official, I felt a sense of something close to relief that it was all over. I never expected to feel that way about the England captaincy.

It was on the Sunday afternoon that a phone call reached me during a friendly, and liberally alcoholic, game of cricket in Oporto. It was a reporter from one of the tabloid dailies and my first reaction was to curse that there was no escape, even while resting up in foreign parts. Anyway, this guy told me that one of the Sunday papers had run a story claiming I had resigned. Speaking instinctively, without any thought for the consequences, I replied that the truth was a shade different, and proceeded to give him the bare bones of my conversation with Ted. When, as his supplementary question, he asked if I had wanted to carry on with the job, I said yes, for no other

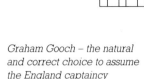

Graham Gooch – the natural and correct choice to assume the England captaincy

reason than that I wanted to get him off the phone and continue my break. It was a mistake.

The following day, doubtless riled by the way in which their rivals had presented this international phone chat with me, another of the tabloids went a step further and dispatched one of its men to find me. I had by this time moved to Dow's Quinta do Bonfim, and I was determined not to have my privacy invaded there, so when this bloke phoned from the town, I reluctantly agreed to talk to him then and there for five minutes so long as, in return, he called off the hunt and went home. When he told me that everyone at home was very excited about the news that I had been sacked when I really wanted to keep the job, an alarm bell rang in my head, warning me that I was getting into very deep water. Suppressing my doubts, I told him how I saw things and rang off, reasoning that I would never have to see his paper anyway.

I returned to England on the Wednesday and went home to await the official verdict. The media were still rampant with speculation about the job, and although Graham Gooch was the bookmakers' favourite now that I was apparently out of the running, six or seven other names were being touted, some with more conviction than others.

By midday on Thursday I had still received no word from HQ, so I turned on my Teletext and discovered that the news was out – 'Goochie' was the new captain, both for the Nehru Cup one-day tournament in India and the full Test tour of the West Indies. It was another two hours before Ted phoned from Lord's to confirm, in short, sharp terms, what I already knew. We had nothing further to say to each other, and although I idly wondered why phoning me had apparently been so low on the priority list, it did not greatly trouble me. The captaincy had ceased to be an issue to me the previous Friday.

For my own convenience, I personally called a press conference at Grace Road. What I had to say was straightforward enough but I had no wish to keep repeating it to anyone who cared to phone. I said it once and then went to ground for the remainder of the day. The gist of my remarks was that I wished Graham well and looked forward to playing under him in the Caribbean. Little did I suspect that, even as I spoke, that contingency was being vetoed by the tour selection committee, meeting at Lord's.

By some quirk of the fixture list, Leicestershire were scheduled to start a four-day home match against Essex the following morning. It was to be Gower against Gooch at the toss-up, old captain against new. It was a natural photograph for the papers and there were more cameras than I have seen for years at Grace Road. The 'snappers' had come to cover a gently poignant situation; they went away with far more emotional pictures than any of them expected, after the news which filtered through during the morning.

The tour parties had been finalised the previous afternoon and evening but I cannot say if anyone tried to contact me then, as I was out to dinner. When morning came, I was up and out of the house far earlier than is my habit as I had a pre-match meeting planned with Mike Turner, and I was in his office, discussing various club issues, when someone poked his head around the door to tell me Ted Dexter was on the phone. As I walked across the corridor to the phone in Mike's secretary's office, it never even crossed my mind that I was about to hear such devastating news. I don't know what I expected Ted to say – it was, after all, early morning and my brain was not yet functioning to capacity – but I imagined it was some minor matter about the handover of captaincy. What he actually said came as much more than a gentle surprise.

Ted told me I was not included in the party to go to the West Indies. He spoke clinically – not that there is ever an easy way of breaking such news. I could not believe what I was hearing. Composing myself, I asked him for the reasons and he said something about batting inconsistency and shoulder injuries. By then, I was not really taking much in as I had gathered there was no single persuasive reason, or at least not one that he was prepared to tell me.

Of course, I had been dropped by England more than once before. But on those occasions it had been signposted, usually by a loss of form and a quiet word from the captain or chairman. This time there was no warning and absolutely no expectation because, although the Australian series had been a personal disaster in one sense, and not one of my best with the bat, I did not feel I had batted that badly. In all my agonising over whether to resign the captaincy, there had always been the consolation that I would still be on the plane to the Caribbean. And now this, a bolt from the blue with which I simply could not come to terms.

I put down the phone, went back into the office and resumed my meeting. My face was blank and I said nothing about the bombshell which had just been dropped at my feet. No one asked, presumably because no one expected it. They were to find out soon enough.

Graham arrived. He looked concerned, as well he might – it cannot have been easy for him as we go back a long way as team-mates and tour friends. We were, I assumed, the only two people on the ground who knew, and when he asked if we could have a private chat, I was only too eager to

Micky Stewart – an obvious party to the decision to leave me out of the touring party completely

agree. He talked me through the thinking as best he could and I appreciated his honesty on what must have been an embarrassing matter. A week earlier, I had been his England captain; now, here he was telling me I was no longer wanted in his England team. A tangled web, indeed.

It was raining, symbolically. There was time to kill and, now that the news was out officially, I agreed to speak to the press boys who had gathered at the foot of the dressing room steps. I am sure my sense of dejection was transparent. I knew the right, proper things to say, and I said them automatically, but I was careful to speak slowly to make sure my voice did not give up on me. I felt genuinely emotional and probably looked it, too, but I had no desire to be added to the list of characters who publicly break down when things go wrong. I got through the ordeal and then retreated, grateful to be alone with my thoughts.

When the weather relented late in the day, we had to go out and field. I am well aware that I set no sort of example to my players, but I think and hope they understood. I was mentally miles away, wondering what on earth I had done to deserve being judged suddenly incapable. Nothing in life is sacred, but I did feel I had done enough to hang on to my place – and with it, my dignity.

I sought no company that evening, because I knew I would be no real company for anyone. The following morning I forced myself to make a resolution. I knew that to malinger for another day would be fatal, and that if I kept feeling so sorry for myself I would walk round looking a zombie and a fool. If for nobody but myself, I had to put on a show. And so I raced around in the field, deliberately looked happier than I felt, and somehow managed to cheer myself up a shade.

It did not last. The lowest moment of all came in the evening session, when I went in to bat. I was determined to make a score, to make a point that would be taken down and used in evidence. Instead, I got a good ball from Derek Pringle which darted back into my pads and I was out lbw for nought. I trailed miserably back to the dressing room, took off all my gear and ran a bath. Then I lay in it for fifteen minutes, a solitary confinement with my confusion and dismay.

At least, before that match and the season came to a close, I did manage to restore much of my own self-belief with a hundred in the second innings. At times when things do not appear to be going your way, these innings mean a lot to a cricketer and can save him from over-dramatic thoughts about his immediate future, on or off the field.

CHAPTER EIGHT

Taking Stock

As I surveyed the winter months stretching ahead of me, only one thing was certain: I would be playing no serious cricket. Once I had come to terms with this unexpected and unwanted vacuum, I determined to make the best of it and use the time available to resolve the pressing issues of my life. Heaven knows, there were enough to keep me busy.

A series of important decisions had to be taken. They did not all concern cricket. My private life was in turmoil, demanding attention for the sake of all involved. Whatever was decided in this sphere could not be seen in isolation, as it would have an inevitable bearing on the future direction of my cricket career. My head swam with the complexity of it all, and it was to be months before I reached all the conclusions and taken the necessary, painful steps to close one long chapter of my life and begin another, totally afresh.

Once the 1989 season was finally out of the way, the last of the perennial benefit games played and the farewells said to county team-mates as they prepared to disperse around the world, my first priority was to organise a suitable date for the operation on my troublesome shoulder. However much I had resisted the idea at the time, it was now clear to me that my batting technique had been compromised, if only subconsciously. I had been like a bird instinctively protecting an injured wing. I was aware of it far more as the season neared its close. It needed time to get tolerably loose, and in routine games where the adrenalin failed to pump, it took much longer. The operation was essential and I booked 14 October for my hospital admission.

There was just time, before that, to squeeze in the first of my brief but eventful winter trips. I was off to Hong Kong, a place I have come to know and like over the years, with a team representing the Lord's Taverners. I had been overseas with the Taverners once before, a memorable jaunt to Berlin, and this expedition followed the established pattern of my currently chaotic life and refused to pass off as quietly as I had planned it. In fact, either side of two games of cricket, sharing the field with prominent old players such as M.J.K. Smith and Faroukh Engineer plus cricketing celebrities such as Tim Rice, I contrived to suffer a bad dose of food poisoning and to miss the flight home!

Food poisoning had been pure bad luck; missing the plane was slightly careless as myself, Bill Wiggins and Christopher Blake allowed ourselves a little leeway before arriving at our departure gate to find that our plane had loaded inordinately quickly and already departed. Mild surprise turned to indignation as we negotiated with Cathay Pacific's ground staff and attempted to find three suitable seats on the next flight to London, fortunately scheduled only two hours later. Only after a quick reassessment of our tactics and the adoption of true humility in deference to the Chinese psyche did we achieve our aim and were rewarded with a very comfortable flight home at the front of the bus.

No sooner back in England, than off to hospital. It was the same one, in north London, where I had undergone the investigative arthroscopy in June – a comfortable place with excellent staff. For all that, it was impossible not to feel a touch nervous. Accepting the need for surgery is one thing; actually approaching the idea of having your shoulder sliced open and bits of floating bone scraped out is quite another. It was something which had to be suffered, certainly not something to look forward to.

It was not until I arrived at the pre-med stage, just outside the operating theatre, that it occurred to me that the surgeon might kill two birds with one knife. I was suffering from Dupytren's Contractions, a condition which affects the fingers and palm of the hand – in effect drawing the fingers in towards the palm until eventually they close up completely unless treated. I quickly weighed up the prospect of waking up with two areas of my body immobilised, decided it was preferable to going through this process twice and asked the surgeon if he could address the two problems at one sitting.

So it was that I came round, some hours later, feeling as helpless as I can ever remember. Drains were running from my shoulder and hand while drips were connected up to my toes and right arm. I had one foot and one arm free. I was very sore and felt as if I was being put through a particulary gruesome kind of torture. Fortunately, I was not obliged to spend too long in this undignified position. Soon, I was passed into the tender care of the hospital physiotherapist. We laughed together as the first set of prescribed exercises proved I could not lift my arm an inch; while laughing, I tried not to cry with the pain.

A combination of tablets and time took the pain away. The champagne, sent in by thoughtful friends, also played its part in this direction. After five days I was pronounced fit enough to face the outside world, if not the West Indian pace attack, and made a gingerly emergence to confront the next phase of the winter, something which was to give me a different kind of pain, mental rather than physical but every bit as acute.

My personal life had to be sorted out. I could not put it off any longer. For twelve years I had been with the same girl, Vicki Stewart, and for the best part of that time we had been living together. We had become engaged and I had bought her the ring to prove it, but somehow marriage had always been something to consider next year rather than this. Now, I knew that I was not going to marry her at all and it was time to call it a day on a sometimes turbulent but mostly very pleasant relationship with a very lovely girl. It could not be easy, and it certainly wasn't but I was aware that to make the break would also make it easier, indeed, more attractive, to leave Leicestershire and make a fresh cricketing start, too – then I would be starting the new decade with what amounted to a new identity. It was an appealing idea, increasingly a compulsive one, but I intended to do nothing in a rush. It was all far too important to decide on purely emotional grounds.

Leicestershire were aware of my dilemma. At least, Mike Turner was aware of it, which to me is the same thing. This was far from being the first time that Mike had heard rumours of my imminent depature, but on all the previous occasions I had been able to refute them, honestly and firmly. I had never wanted to leave; part of me did not want to leave now, either, but Mike appreciated my position, right down to the pressing personal situation, and although he made it plain that he wanted me to stay with the club and remain as captain, he deliberately stood back and applied no pressure.

One minor interference came with some unfortunate remarks about my style of captaincy, attributed to our club chairman Don Tebbutt in a newspaper not generally renowned for the accuracy of its quotes. The chairman sought to reassure me that his words had been taken out of context, but I was not over-concerned. It made no difference at all to my thinking.

If a county club is going to operate at all smoothly, the captain and chief executive need to work closely together. Once that becomes impossible, everyone at the club will suffer for it. In the years I had been Leicestershire's captain, my understanding with Mike had improved enormously. I am sure there were times in my younger days when we exasperated each other but now, I believed, we worked well together. Many times I had been aware of his support for me, not just on Grace Road affairs, but also at Lord's when the Test and County Cricket Board had debated various issues of my career, not least the England captaincy. Mike and I had become close, as friends as well as professional colleagues, and the most difficult thing facing me as I considered my future with or without Leicestershire was to isolate myself from the emotional loyalty.

I elected to take one thing at a time. The captaincy had to be first because the county committee traditionally meets in November to appoint or reappoint for the following year. They needed to know and I told them, through Mike, that I did not wish to continue.

Of all the reasoning which went in to this decision, the most persuasive factor was my sense of disappointment with the response I had had from the dressing room during the past summer. I had often been away with England, a contingency which was fully appreciated when the committee launched me on a second term in the job in 1988; in my absences, I wanted to think that things would run relatively smoothly and that I would be able to slip back into the side at the end of a Test Match without having to resolve an accumulation of niggles. In practice, this was hard to achieve even with the best of intentions. For some years now, Leicestershire have underachieved on the field. We have had a playing staff of considerable ability but this has never translated into tangible success. In 1989 the shortcomings were more acute than ever. We had a wretchedly disappointing season in all four major competitions and I found it frustratingly difficult to know why.

What I did know, with sinking certainty, was that I was finding it impossible to sustain a happy dressing room, especially from a distance during England games. I have never been one to phone the club several times a day during a Test match. While with England, I believed that I should be concentrating on the game at hand and leaving county affairs in the hands of deputies appointed for the purpose. I also, perhaps, tend to take it as read that professional sportsmen will behave in a professional way, whether or not their captain is watching over them. This, apparently, took too much for granted.

Every county dressing room endures its petty niggles. Although the Leicester dressing room was full of talented players and likeable characters, some of these problems had reached a point where something had to give. It came to a head during a match at Scarborough, while I was once again absent on international duty. The game had nothing much riding on it but we happened to get into a position to win, which was rare enough that summer to be an incentive in itself. Unfortunately our overseas player, the West Indian Winston Benjamin, then proceeded to bowl in such a desultory way as to give the clear impression that he, at least, did not care about the result one way or the other. We lost the game and all hell broke loose back in the dressing room.

I spoke privately with 'Benjy'. He is a cricketer who does try his best, almost invariably, and he had produced telling performances through the season with the frequency one would expect from the club's star overseas player. His reaction, when tackled, was that in the course of the season there had been times when certain others had not tried as hard as they

94

might, without such a spectacular furore. If there was a simple solution, it eluded me. I talked with all the other prime figures in the dispute, and then I addressed the team as a whole, yet I was uncomfortably aware that a legacy of ill-feeling remained. It depressed me. I felt that if I could not keep the side together, sorting out such difficulties as they arose, then I was better off without all the hassle that the captaincy entailed.

I have often thought that it is not commonly appreciated just what a taxing job county captaincy can be. It is, in some ways, harder than captaining a Test team, where you have a greater depth of quality players at your disposal and you do not suffer the inevitable irritations which arise whenever a group of disparate men are obliged to live in each other's pockets. County captains, I had discovered, are a much-stressed breed, and it was partly this background knowledge which told me the time had come to stand back and be a little more selfish, concentrating on my own career without worrying so much about other people.

Mike Turner expressed his disappointment. Something tells me that Nigel Briers, who inherited the job, did not regard it as cause for unconfined joy, either. But, for me, it was another part of the jigsaw completed, if in a somewhat negative way.

Christmas was coming and I was off to South Africa – not to play cricket, nor to have any direct dealings with the cricket authorities, but to combine a couple of speaking engagements with the self-indulgence of a week in the bush. I packed the black tie and dinner jacket, a few appropriate items for

My first winter decision was to give up the captaincy of Leicestershire. I then had to ponder whether to leave Grace Road, my only home in 15 years of county cricket

beach trips and my camera for the game reserves. I set off alone, leaving behind a home in which the atmosphere was now increasingly and understandably strained between two people well aware that their years together were drawing to a close.

I spoke at a banquet given by the Kent Park Taverners in Johannesburg, and then at a meeting of the Oaks Club in Cape Town. Along the way I caught up with some old friends, such as Paddy Clift, a long-time team-mate at Grace Road, and Robin Jackman, not at home in Cape Town but at Johannesburg airport, heading back to England for a flying visit. I had one memorable dinner party with some of the great names of South African cricket – Clive Rice, Vince van der Bijl and Graeme Pollock. Way back in 1965 I had attended a Test match for the first time. It was at Trent Bridge, against South Africa, and Pollock scored 125. I was only eight years of age but this powerful left-hander made a great impression on me and became a hero. Years later, I was to fulfil an ambition by batting with him, during the international festival at Jesmond. He made another century. Now, at last, I was getting to know him socially and finding he lived up to all expectations.

Then it was off to the bush – to Londolozi, a game farm near the Kruger National Park, run by the Varty brothers who had looked after me famously on a previous visit. I stayed in one of the bungalows on the compound, which stretches picturesquely down to a river and through which, unplanned and

slightly disconcertingly, some of the wild animals wander. I had a Land Rover and a tracker to accompany me morning and evening, and I took countless pictures of leopards, lions, cheetahs, elephants and rhino. Best of all, I revelled in the solitude and escapism of this magical world, and vowed to return again at the first opportunity.

Despite the enjoyment of the trip, I felt low when I returned home. It was no longer my omission by England which depressed me; I had got over that blow and even pushed ahead with plans to travel independently to the Caribbean, working for *The Times* newspaper and for BBC Radio. No, it was on the personal front that I was now feeling melancholy, knowing what had to be done yet dreading the process.

Just before Christmas, only a few days after my return from South Africa, the *Daily Express* managed to make things even worse. They devoted much of their front page to a picture of Vicki and me, 'in happier times', and an accompanying story which asserted a number of things, among them: (1) that we had split up, (2) that I had bought a house in Hampshire, and (3) that I had just got back from Kenya. It was a misinformed piece on almost every count, but by some mischance their biggest punt – on the break-up – was effectively true. We had been intent on saying nothing publicly until we were both ready, but this story activated the newshounds of other papers and our peaceful home in Leicester came under seige. I was able to say that we were sharing Christmas, which at least cast some delaying doubt in prying minds. We did spend the holiday together, too, though I do not think either of us would claim it was the most joyful Christmas of our lives. Once it was over, we reviewed our situations and decided that, largely because I was planning to go to St Moritz early in the New Year, we should make an announcement. Some clever reporter would be bound to notice that I had again gone away alone and Vicki, left in the house while she found somewhere new to live, might easily have been put under yet more pressure.

For our final act together, we at least carried it off in some style. We chose *The Times* personal columns, on New Year's Day, to make a joint announcement of our separation. The motive behind it was purely to draw the fire of the media, and, to some degree, it succeeded. There was little left for them to ask now that the secret was out in the open.

Unfortunately, this chaotic winter refused to leave us in peace. Unplanned and unwanted events in St Moritz brought me very reluctantly back into the public spotlight. My attempts to lead a normal life were failing, week by week.

> **DAVID** Gower and Vicky Stewart Would like to put themselves and their friends out of their misery and confirm that sadly they have decided to separate as amicably as possible and go their own ways. As the matter has already been the subject of speculation by some members of the Press, they hope that this brief announcement will obviate the need for further comment. (Fat...chance!).

CHAPTER NINE

Making the Break

I f I needed any confirmation of my state of mind, it came on the Cresta Run. I had gone out there hoping, as ever, to improve my personal best on the run. Instead, I found myself recording times of about a second and a half slower than when I was last there. And yet, after a few days in convivial company, including my regular running-mate Allan Lamb, I began to perk up and take an interest in life once more. It was then that I parked a hired car in the lake and set off yet more bizarre and unwelcome publicity.

The *Daily Mirror* had sent out a reporter and a photographer to do a picture story of me on the Cresta. They were both well known to me, through cricket, and on the Saturday night of our stay we went out to dinner together, along with the two sons of Lynn Wilson, Allan Lamb's county chairman at Northamptonshire. After dinner we moved on to the King's Club, a well-known night spot in St Moritz, and what with one thing and another it was pretty late when we decided to head for our beds. Feeling in higher spirits than for some considerable time, I decided we should avoid the main roads and drive across the lake. Call it reckless if you like, but I was aware that the ice was thick enough to support a car; I was also under the impression that it was perfectly legal, and only discovered later that the lake had been ruled out of bounds to motor vehicles a few years earlier.

The good news is that we negotiated the ice safely enough and dropped off the *Mirror* boys at their hotel. The bad news is that I decided I should have just a little more fun before the night was out. So I nosed the hired Opel back on to the lake and, this time, drove across it instead of up and down. I thought I knew the geography well enough, and as I reached the far side I was looking for the ramp which is erected during the polo season, allowing cars to park on the ice. Unfortunately, I was a month too soon – the polo had not yet begun and there was no ramp. I swung the car round and headed back the way I had come – or so I thought.

By now, it seems, my sense of direction had begun to desert me and I was actually heading for the perilous area at the point of the lake where it is joined by the river. Here, the ice is conspicuously thinner. I did not come upon it entirely without warning – I spotted in the headlights a different shade to the ice – but realising the danger was one thing, avoiding it quite another. Braking on ice and snow is far from straightforward, and as the front wheels cracked the ice, bringing me to a crunching tilting halt, there was, I will admit, a touch of panic inside the car. It did not seem a very attractive way to go.

The car came cosily to rest, its nose buried in the water, the tail still sitting on the solid ice. Very quickly it was an empty car, as I scrambled out, waded through a foot of water to get back on to the ice and then stood, feeling a shade foolish and a little uncertain of what to do next.

Nobody was going to come to my rescue at that hour of the night, so my fate was in my own hands. Having by now conquered the instant fear of sinking, I calmly opened the boot, took out the ski bags and headed off across the lake towards the town. It was a half-hour's slithering walk and when I got there it soon became clear that I was not going to get the car rescued until morning. The taxi drivers outside the Palace Hotel told me of a garage that would be opening at 7.30 a.m. and might have a tow-truck. It was all I could hope for.

Before turning in for the night, a little fraught but with that surging sense of relief that accompanies the realisation of a narrow escape, I had one final look back across the lake. The Opel was as I had left it, resting at a drunken angle, bathed in moonlight.

I booked a call for 7.15 a.m. but slept through it. When I awoke it was 9.15, and hurrying down to the lobby I detailed a search party of hotel staff. They soon returned with the news I had half-feared. There was now no car on the lake. It was beyond the help of a tow-truck.

This called for some serious assessment of my position. It was not an enviable one. Things might have been tricky enough with an abandoned vehicle parked on thin ice; it would have taken some explaining. Now however, the only visible evidence of my misadventure was some tyre tracks leading to a hole in the ice, and footprints leaving the scene. The St Moritz constabulary would be failing in their duty if they turned a communal blind eye. On top of this, there was the question of the car-hire company, whose reaction to the news that one of their vehicles could be collected from the bottom of the lake was unlikely to be one of sanguine resignation.

What was required, it seemed to me, was some sound legal advice. I soon discovered that a Cresta member by the name of Urs Nater was a lawyer who happened to be setting up a practice in St Moritz. It was not difficult to track him down and, having listened to my story, his unsurprising instruction was that we should inform both the police and the rental company before they were tempted to concoct their own version of events.

The police, it transpired, had already been to the scene and formed the opinion that there was more than one set of footprints. When the press inevitably got wind of the story, this fuelled their salacious imaginations. So far as they were concerned, there must have been a 'mystery blonde' involved, and they were not easily to be persuaded otherwise.

All of which conspired to ensure that the St Moritz police received a level of interest from the British press that they can seldom have experienced, while D. Gower received further notoriety which was not only unwanted but, in the case of the female connection, unmerited. And as I extricated myself from the mess with the promise of returning to meet all salvage costs, the press directed their most probing questions at the one person who knew nothing about the affair – Vicki, back home in Leicester. Not unnaturally, she responded with rather bad grace. On my return, the atmosphere was still more strained than it had been when I left.

The only thing that could possibly be said in favour of all this was that my absence from England's intensive tour preparations was causing me no grief. By the time I returned to England, the two England squads – one to tour the Caribbean, the other a 'reserve' side heading for Zimbabwe – had convened at the National Sports Centre, at Lilleshall in Shropshire. I recalled my conversation with Ted Dexter and Micky Stewart, during the meeting at which they made it plain that my captaincy days were over. I remembered stressing my view that the lateness of the tour to the West Indies made it crucial that the chosen players should spend some time together, to improve both their fitness and their readiness to tackle such a series as a united group. I was glad it was happening, but I was not too worried that it was taking place without me. Any envy I might have felt had now gone, absorbed by the apparently endless series of problems which had queued up to complicate my winter.

There was also the undeniable fact that, even if I had been mentally fit to tackle a tour – which was doubtful – I was not physically fit. Without the pressing January deadline as an incentive, I had deliberately allowed my shoulder to recover in its own time. I had not pushed it and it was still a long way short of being free and comfortable enough to contemplate playing cricket.

What I did have to contemplate, and soon, was exactly where I would be playing my cricket in future. Having made the split with Vicki, I think I knew in my own mind that I would be leaving Leicestershire in search of a fresh start; I think I had also narrowed my options down to two.

A number of counties had made informal, unofficial approaches to me, usually through a friend on their staff. It was as if they were just testing the water, going through the motions, and in almost every instance I was able to thank them for their interest and decline to pursue it. I had decided that my next, and hopefully last, county employers would be either Kent or Hampshire.

Both clubs had gone through the correct channels to register their official interest. With Leicestershire's permission, I had spoken to Jim Woodhouse, chairman of Kent's cricket committee, and Hampshire's chief executive Tony Baker, discussing options and seeking common ground. Neither man had tried to rush me into a decision, doubtless because they had been warned by their respective captains that this would be the quickest way to alienate me.

Chris Cowdrey, the Kent captain, and Mark Nicholas, his counterpart at Hampshire, are both good friends of mine. They are also very friendly with each other, so there was scope for plenty of good-natured rivalry, and I can imagine the phone lines between Canterbury and Southampton were kept pretty busy as Cowdrey and Nicholas tried to find out how the other was progressing with negotiations.

The truth, for some while, was that neither made any significant progress because I retreated within myself to try to reach a conclusion I would not come to regret. It took longer than I had planned. There were many factors in favour of going to Kent – so many that, in the final reckoning, it may have counted against them. To begin with, I was born in Tunbridge Wells; I spent nine years going to school in the county, first at Marlborough House, Hawkhurst, and then King's Canterbury. I still have friends and contemporaries in the area, not the least of them being Chris Cowdrey himself.

We are the same age, Chris and I, and we go back a long way. In 1976 I played under his captaincy for Young England in the Caribbean. Nine years later I was his England captain in India, where he played all five Tests. We have always had a great rapport and I would like to have played a few years' county cricket with him. It was a strong temptation.

All these factors combined led most people to assume that Kent was my logical choice. Being of a somewhat perverse nature, I may then have developed a wish to do the opposite. I looked more closely at the Hampshire option, and liked what I saw. There was little doubt in my mind that Hampshire were the stronger team. They had a particularly talented batting line-up, and the prospect of batting regularly with Robin Smith, as I had done for England the previous summer, was very appealing.

Wherever I chose to go, I wanted it to be within striking distance of London, where many of my closest friends are based. Hampshire fitted the bill there, too, and it is a county I had always enjoyed visiting. Another mark

Eventually I managed to come to a decision to join Hampshire and their captain, Mark Nicholas

in their favour was that, rightly or wrongly, I felt I needed to go to a club which might help me as much as I would help them. After a miserable season in 1989, Kent undeniably had problems and there was a danger that too much might have been expected of me. Hampshire already had star names in residence and title ambitions on hold. To join them in trying to bring those ambitions to fruition seemed to suit my purposes better than trying to create something new at Canterbury.

If I was close to a decision, however, it was not going to be made without a serious sense of regret over leaving Leicester. Even after months of agonising I had not entirely come to terms with the wrench. Naturally, I had a great many friends in Leicester. I also had, indeed currently still have, a very pleasant home which I was loath to abandon. Leicester had given me my one fixed asset in life; I liked the place and its people. Moreover, I had no direct row with the club. It was abundantly clear, however, that most people expected me to go, reasoning that to stay on, under a new captain and after all that had recently occurred in my life, would put me in an untenable position. For me, any temptation to stay on was also counteracted by a suspicion that I had been rooted too long, I had a hankering to find out what cricket life was like elsewhere, and I knew that now, when a three-year contract somewhere would lead me conveniently to an age of contentment, was the time to do it.

I had still made nothing official when, in mid January, I motored down to Hertfordshire to spend a week at Champneys, the health resort. Towards the end of the summer I had agreed to feature in an advert for them, never reckoning on the fact that it would be prominently displayed in the *Daily Telegraph* on the first morning of the final Test match, under the heading: 'I wish I was at Champneys . . .'. How anyone in the game could genuinely interpret this as a show of uninterest on my part is beyond me, but some did, and another furore of the storm-in-a-teacup variety ensued. Part of my deal for the advert, however, had been a complimentary weekend at the resort, to be used whenever I chose. I decided to turn it into a week's stay and regard it as the launch of my personal winter training programme. I worked well with their physio, a man named Dave Barton and, ironically, an Australian, and by the time I emerged at the end of the week I felt more relaxed than I had done in some while, in addition to being a shade fitter.

Perhaps the peaceful environment at Champneys, and the absence of external pressures, had helped to concentrate my mind. I certainly knew it was time for a decision. I phoned Mark Nicholas and told him that I wanted to join him at Hampshire. He was gratifyingly pleased. I then phoned Mike Turner and arranged to see him at Grace Road the next morning. He was not going to be pleased, and I braced myself for what I knew would be a

The player and the journalist – an early
investigative conversation with Allan
Lamb in Jamaica

Graham Gooch reduced to a passive
role in Barbados after his earlier
successes

(*top opposite*) Showing willing in
Guyana

(*bottom opposite*) Graham Gooch's
broken hand is the cause of my
temporary call-up to play in Barbados

(*below*) A change of environment! Filing
a report from the Jamaica press box

Apparently relaxed against Barbados –
but sadly unproductive!

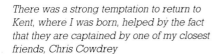

difficult meeting.

It felt strange that January morning, driving in to Grace Road for the last time as an employee of the club. For so many years, it had been such an accepted part of my life. I knew everyone at the club as a friend, and there was little about me that the staff did not know. For all the problems there had been on the field, the frustrations of having a talented team which failed to achieve and individuals who sometimes failed to co-exist, it had been home for a very long time and I felt a strong sense of loyalty to the people I was about to leave behind.

But it had to be done; there was no going back. Mike accepted the news with disappointment, though no great surprise. He had wanted me to stay but, I suspect, never really believed that I would once I had given up the captaincy. He wished me well and we parted on very good terms, sure to remain friends even at a distance.

It was not, at first, an easy thing to live with. I received a lot of letters, virtually all of which expressed dismay at my departure. None was angry or recriminatory. People seemed to understand why I had to go, which, in a funny way, added to the poignancy of it. I hope I shall always retain my fond memories of Grace Road, no matter what the future has in store.

And now it was the future I had to address. If this was a sad end to one phase of my career, I still had a great deal to play for. In the course of a year, even slightly less, everything that could happen to me had done so. I needed to start again, and with that knowledge came lingering doubts. If I am honest, I felt a slight fear of the unknown, and I was well aware that to succeed, I needed to be more positive about my cricket and my life in general than ever I had been before.

It all looks so friendly, doesn't it? England's start in the Caribbean on the delightful island of St Kitts

CHAPTER TEN

The Pen and the Microphone

I would be fooling nobody if I pretended it felt totally natural to stroll into the environment of an England tour in the unfamiliar guise of a journalist. The circumstances in which I had been omitted from the playing party, and the personalities involved in that decision, gave grounds for a degree of embarrassment on both sides and I must admit to a sense of trepidation as I set off from Heathrow Airport bound for Kingston, Jamaica and my contracted assignments for *The Times* and BBC Radio.

There was plenty of time for me to ponder all the possibilities. Too much time by far, as problems with my connecting flight enforced a long wait at Miami airport while Air Jamaica tried to locate the aircraft which was to ferry us down to Kingston. Tired and frustrated when I finally checked into the Pegasus Hotel at 3 a.m., my one consolation was that I had made my

entry at a time of night when I did not have to worry about bumping into anyone. I crept off to my bed for a well-earned sleep, and the following morning there was a gratifying normality about the long sequence of reunions. Any threat of embarrassment, any hint of strangeness, dissipated in no time as, one by one, I ran into players and press people in the hotel lobby. It was, in most cases, just like any meeting with old friends, and the welcome I received from my closest pals in the team, Allan Lamb and Graham Gooch, routinely broke the ice.

It would not quite be true to say that I had no further cause for discomfort during my stay, but from that morning on I had no serious reservations about the wisdom of taking up the option of commentating on a tour I had hoped and believed I would be playing in. It had not, after all, been a straight-forward commercial decision. When *The Times* approached me, I had had to weigh up the situation very carefully. Would I be seen as intruding in an area from which I had consciously been excluded? Would the antipathy with which I had come to regard certain newspaper writers during the past summer make my presence in the press box reciprocally sensitive? On the other hand, I did want to explore the avenues of broadcasting and writing, with my future in mind. I also enjoy the Caribbean. I accepted the offer and hoped for the best.

My first day in Kingston was hectic. Not only did I write my first piece for *The Times*, without any 'ghosting' assistance, I also indulged myself socially, had my first strenuous exercise since the shoulder operation, re-estab-lished a friendly relationship with Micky Stewart and, at the very end, got myself run over. And to think I had travelled to the Caribbean hoping life might quieten down for a while!

For both our sakes, it was useful to have an early chat with Micky. We had not spoken since that long-ago Friday at Ted's house when it was made plain to me that my time as England captain was over. There had been no word from him when I was left out of the tour team and I was still in the dark about the real reasons for it. Micky had obviously been a party to the de-cision, and now was a good time to clear the air and put it all behind us.

Our meeting was virtually arranged for us. Before leaving England, the Test and Country Cricket Board had been in touch, asking if I would mind ferrying out some urgent supplies for Allan Lamb (surprisingly not cham-pagne) and a bagful of match balls to deliver to Micky. The balls brought us together.

Micky came to my hotel room on that first night. If there was any sense of slight embarrassment on his side, he did not show it, and after a few minutes of general, light-hearted banter he brought up the touchy subject of team selection and made an effort to explain the thinking. It was largely going over familiar ground and he shed no new light on the matter, insisting that my fitness was their primary concern. The fact that my shoulder was, at that moment, aching after an exploratory game of tennis with Graham Gooch was only a semi-vindication for them because I still believed I could have advanced my fitness programme if the tour incentive had been my target. Nevertheless, now was not the moment to protest. I was beyond that stage. The manager and I finished our discussion amicably, and for the remainder of my time in the Caribbean we got along in a perfectly relaxed way. I did not, on that jet-lagged evening in Jamaica, expect that our relationship would be a professional one again within a matter of weeks.

The peculiarity of being a pressman with special affinities among the players might have come home to me later that same evening, when I accompanied Lamb and Gooch to a party thrown by a Jamaican we had met on the previous tour. Several of the younger England players also came

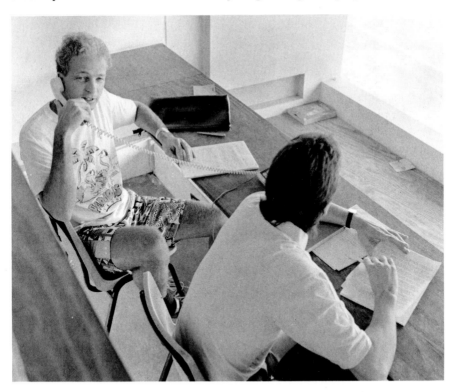

Suitably relaxed in Jamaica – not having to face the West Indies attack and filing my first preview for The Times

Angus Fraser, the key bowler at Sabina Park, acclaims another wicket with Alec Stewart's plain approval

along but none of them seemed to worry about my presence among them or, heaven forbid, to see me as any sort of 'security risk'. It was a very convivial night and as it ended, I wandered into the roadway clutching a glass of rum, and our hostess, reversing her car prior to giving us a lift home, proceeded to run over my foot! I hit the deck in a hurry to try and avoid too much damage, and sadly failed in my attempt to preserve my drink at the same time.

Had I been playing in the First Test match, I would have needed a fitness test at the final practice session the following morning. As it was, my limp was purely a source of amusement as I carried a briefcase rather than a cricket bag into Sabina Park and adjusted to my new duties. The briefcase was not, to be perfectly honest, packed with record books to educate my prose. Rather, it contained such essential Caribbean equipment as a corkscrew and, well, a spare corkscrew. But it did boast a variety of pens and a good supply of writing pads so that, after the ritual inspection of the pitch, I was able to sit down in the well-positioned yet painfully uncomfortable press box and, amid some curiosity, dispatch my preliminary thoughts on the match.

Predictably, they were not entirely optimistic. My previous visit to Kingston, four years earlier, made certain of that. In 1986 Sabina Park had been the graveyard of our hopes and plans, for all that it was the First Test of the series. The one-day international which preceded it sent Mike Gatting home with a flattened nose; the Test itself was played on a demon of a pitch, its grassy undulations permitting outrageously uneven bounce and making the already hazardous task of confronting four fresh fast bowlers almost intolerably dangerous. One can only estimate the psychological damage we suffered there, not simply from being beaten inside three days but from the style of defeat. My first perusal of this year's pitch comforted me. It did not appear so blatantly brutal. Experience, however, has taught me the folly of being too categorical about pitches.

The match began on a Saturday and, with no piece to write for *The Times*, I was commentating on *Test Match Special* as the West Indies, having won the toss, made their customary sound start. Greenidge and Haynes put on 62 for the first wicket. Normal service, it seemed, was to continue undisturbed – indeed, might well have done so if Greenidge had not misjudged his attempt to make a misfield, at long leg, by Devon Malcolm look even more foolish. It was Greenidge who was made to look the dunce as Malcolm's recovering throw arrived with pinpoint accuracy. From that moment on, the match belonged to England.

West Indies lost all ten first-innings wickets for 102 runs, an incredible sight both for the rarity value of such a batting collapse and for the uniform excellence of the English bowling. It was a pre-ordained policy to play just the four seam bowlers, a tactic which depends heavily on your quartet maintaining high levels of stamina and accuracy. Malcolm, Small, Fraser and Capel achieved the aim admirably, their rigid line restricting the batsmen and forcing some of them into injudicious shots in an attempt to break the shackles.

Malcolm was the quickest, Small and Capel were brisk and persistent, but Fraser emerged as the undoubted star by taking the last five wickets for 6 runs and extinguishing any prospect of the kind of low-order rally with which the West Indies have frustrated us on so many previous occasions.

Before the Test there had been those who would have left out Fraser following his evident loss of control in the match against Jamaica. It was, however, a time for selectors to back the qualities of the player as perceived over a longer time-scale and, rightly, there was little problem in placing his name on the team-sheet. Fraser's first spell proved the Jamaica episode to have been no more than a temporary lapse and he effectively blocked up an end. His most testing moment, mentally, came with the first ball of his next spell, when Jack Russell's take in front of first slip was not enough to convince the umpire that Viv Richards had got a touch. Richards, intent on dominating but not in prime form, hit Fraser for two consecutive fours but a potentially pivotal phase ended in an over-ambitious pull against Malcolm. The decks were now cleared, and 'Gus' cleaned up.

As I took a taxi down to Sabina for the second day's play, the man on the radio was muttering darkly about the whole of the Caribbean being in a state of shock after Saturday's events. It was good to hear, the boot too often having been on the other foot, but I have to admit I would have felt it all the more rewarding had I been one of the chosen eleven on the field. Delighted though I was, especially for my close friends in the side, that things had begun so well, human nature insisted that I was also experiencing an uncomfortable jealousy. These mixed feelings were heightened on day two as England, banishing the general fear that the West Indies' pace bowlers would reclaim the lost ground, established a match-winning lead. Lamb's century was brilliant. He appears to thrive on West Indian bowling while others perish to it, and the one surprising fact about his innings was that it was his first overseas Test century, on his sixth full tour. If it was a

RIGHT: Devon Malcolm wins this duel with Viv Richards and England move closer to victory

FAR RIGHT: 'The huddle'. Graham Gooch's final words before the day's play

personal breakthrough, it was a very timely one.

By the close of that second day, England were 342 for 8 and I left the ground pondering profound thoughts on how people react under unaccustomed pressure. In the case of Viv Richards, the West Indies captain, the answer was not very well. Richards is much more used to being in a position of dominance through the power of his bowling attack, and his uncertainty showed. Now that he was forced on to the defensive, he liberally adopted the stable-door-and-bolting-horse philosophy, shifting his fielders in pursuit of the last shot. He also bowled his spinners far too long, to no effect and at a time when England were still vulnerable to a strike from the quick men. He had spread his fields so wide by this stage, however, that the batsmen were able to accumulate singles as they desired. Richards' tactics should surely have followed the English strategy on the opening day, persevering with his main attack to a tight-set field. But then, as I was rapidly discovering, the game does seem easier from the cool elevations of the press and commentary boxes.

England extended their lead to 200 on the third morning and then effectively won the game by reducing West Indies to 229 for 8. Only while Richards and Carlisle Best were together, putting on 80 for the fifth wicket, was England's grip remotely loosened, and when Malcolm, whose

accuracy was a revelation to me as to many others, took Richards' wicket for the second time in the game with an inswinging yorker, the issue was settled. Indeed, a three-day finish, totally reversing the events of 1986, was only narrowly avoided.

The rest day was to follow and, as is usual in the Caribbean, the Test match sponsors, Cable and Wireless, staged a reception for players, officials and press on the evening prior to the free day. Never, in my experience, has one of these parties been held in such an unimaginable atmosphere, which even Gooch's determinedly understated comments

about 'three good days' could not dissipate. It needed something extraordinary to deny England now, and as the rain poured down on Kingston during the rest day and the following morning, we all feared that it was about to happen. We were to learn, as the tour progressed, that it now seems to rain everywhere in the West Indies, usually at the most inconvenient times to England. This time, however, it ceased in time, and although the fourth day was totally lost, the job was finished before lunch on the fifth.

Briefly, I was in a turmoil. This was a historic moment, an unthinkable

Fraser's delight in the Test turns to despair three days later as Ian Bishop hits the last ball of the one-day international for four

victory, one of which I would have loved to be a part. But it had to be faced that I was not, and as I gazed down on the celebrations from the far side of the ground, I asked myself how best to respond. Should I stay away from the players completely? Should I just put my head around the door, say 'well done' and leave them to it? I chose the latter course but was given no chance to pursue it. The party back at the hotel was already under way when I strolled in and I was made instantly welcome, so much so that I found myself being the last one to leave. It was a memorable day, a wonderful atmosphere, and, despite all the pangs of envy, I felt nothing but delight and admiration for Graham Gooch.

In the cold light of day, of course, I had to make sense of what people were already, prematurely, calling a revolution, and to do so while keeping hold of my self-esteem. Under my captaincy, England had been beaten 4 – 0 in a home series the majority had expected them to win. Under the new stewardship of Graham, England had stepped into the cauldron of a Caribbean series, apparently tackled the most difficult Test first, and won it by nine wickets in a little over three days' playing time. How could it happen?

Among the many written post-mortems of the 1989 Ashes series, my eye was caught by an interview with Bob Simpson, Australia's coach and now the manager at my erstwhile county of Leicestershire. In it, Simpson made much of the '2 – 3 per cent solution', by which he explains that players within a team game need only be improved by a relatively small percentage in order to turn a losing side into a winning one. This, I felt, was what had happened in Kingston. It was no miracle, simply one side playing above themselves while the other was below par. England managed to keep their noses in front throughout, and greatly though I admired Lamb's innings, and the support from Robin Smith, it was the bowling which made the essential difference.

The pious talk one often hears about bowlers having 'done their homework' is so much rubbish. Naturally, players talk about the strengths and weaknesses of opposing batsmen, but most of the field-setting intelligence comes out of the captain's head while for the bowlers, no matter who is standing at the other end, the fundamentals remain the same. The 'plan', in its simplest form, is to bowl to a good line and length. It was the same all summer long against Australia, when our bowlers seldom once kept to the script. But in Kingston, all the accuracy and containment for which a captain prays was present throughout.

In Georgetown there was nothing but frustration for the England camp and, particularly, for Micky Stewart, whose job it was to keep all the players occupied amid the rain

So what made the difference? It could be that, for this particular contest, they had happened upon the ideal combination, in which case all credit to the selectors. I tend to believe, however, that the captain must have had some influence, if not a huge one, on the performance of his bowlers. They must have responded to his approach because the atmosphere on the field does emanate from the captain, even if the end result does not. He can set standards and, to a degree, he can inspire, but he must largely rely upon the chosen players creating their own pride and inspiration.

Graham very modestly remarked after the game that there is only so much you can do as a captain and that he had been lucky. He had discovered, as Richards and Clive Lloyd had done before him, that with four very effective fast bowlers in your side, the captaincy job is half-done. He was, however, being excessively self-deprecatory, because it was already very plain to me that Graham was making an indelible mark on this series. He was running the show, as he had done since the original selection meeting when, because it was convened so hurriedly, he may not have come out with exactly the squad he would have chosen himself. As the pre-tour programme proceeded, with the limited-overs Nehru Cup in India a competitive aperitif, Graham grew in confidence as a leader and evidently transmitted this to his players. The obvious difference between his captaincy style and mine is in his approach to training and his determination, despite being older than all except Eddie Hemmings, to be the fittest and fastest. He backs himself against anyone and there are certain positive feelings which come through from that.

Apart from being present and past captains, Graham and I had something else in common as the party moved off from Kingston later that week. Our next destination was Georgetown, Guyana. England had not visited this tip of the South American mainland since 1981. Graham alone has made both trips as a player, but, like him, I was going back with memories which could not be described as fond.

On England's tour of nine years earlier, this destitute, yet once elegant city became famous very quickly, but for political rather than cricketing action. The arrival of Robin Jackman, and his rapid expulsion by the Guyanese government, made headlines around the world, quite apart from jeopardising the tour and, fleetingly, diplomatic relations between the two countries.

The rest of the playing party, Gooch and Gower included, had already spent a week sheltering from persistent rain. We trained indoors, at a sports hall remarkable only for a very high ratio of mosquitoes per cubic foot, most of which, I remember, homed in on John Emburey, while the rest of us tried to avoid being tackled too hard by Ian Botham in the five-a-side football. We managed only two outdoor practice sessions, one on a real cricket pitch and the other on the tarmac of a school playground, while our scheduled four-day match at Bourda was washed away by the weather. We did play a one-day international, but this was staged in the jungle country of Berbice, whence we were whisked by army helicopters. The following day, our manager Alan Smith was actively seeking military aid again as we realised we had to leave the country as fast as possible in the wake of the infamous deportation order served on my old pal 'Jackers'. I left without once setting foot inside Bourda, which, it might fairly be said, was a good reason for going back. I could not think of many others, off-hand.

I had decided to be positive in a very negative way – I told myself that it was certain to be a dreadful twelve days, so that it would seem an unexpected bonus if anything actually went right. By these means, I was able to get through an undoubted ordeal in reasonable shape, despite the fact that – deportation orders aside – it followed a remarkably similar course to the 1981 visit.

This time, we were not even chalked down for a match against the Guyanan side, the organisers presumably deciding that this would give the lads too much of a good thing. Instead, it was straight into the fourth of the one-day games, followed by the Second Test. We got through the international in good style, even if England did play badly enough to make it a no-contest, but the following day I was on familiar territory as the rains began. For five days and nights, it showed no inclination to stop, the upshot being that the Test match was abandoned without a ball bowled.

Anyone who enjoys a life of comfort, with expansive choice of night life, modern facilities and communications, good food and wine, is advised to leave Georgetown out of the reckoning. The people are unfailingly friendly and impressively optimistic, but it is a decayed and depressed city, economically ravaged. Politically it is probably more stable than it had been on my previous visit, but as the rain fell on our welcoming but limited hotel, the days stretched tediously ahead. Books were read, and in some cases written; some unlikely people, myself among them, resorted to some training jogs along the sea wall. For the players deprived of proper practice, let alone actual cricket, it was a huge frustration with which I could intimately sympathise. They had come to Guyana holding the initiative. Who knows what might have happened if they had produced another competent Test-match performance there? Instead, while England stagnated, the West Indies had the chance to regroup.

The decision to abandon the Test was taken on the evening of the rest day, and caused some righteous indignation. I could well see why. Two days playing time remained, and while the prevailing conditions made it

*The Trinidad Test revolved to a large extent
on the outcome of the toss. Gooch won it, and
England all but won the game*

certain that the penultimate day would not start on time, Bourda was drying so fast that play would have been possible at some stage. The substitution of another, unconnected one-day international was ambiguous. If any play at all is possible, a Test match should remain sacred to administrators, as it certainly was to the players who, through this expedient, missed out on a cap, quite apart from some more meaningful cricket.

My own frustrations during the confinement in Georgetown extended to my broadcasting role. In taking my seat at the commentary point for the one 'official' day of cricket during the leg, I discovered a fuming, fraught producer, Peter Baxter, endeavouring to unravel the mystery of why we had no circuit to London. After much vain discussion and a good deal of shrugging, not to mention some minor explosions from the indomitable Mr Baxter, we had to accept that ball-by-ball commentary was impossible. Instead, Christopher Martin-Jenkins made a valiant attempt to keep British listeners in touch on a telephone which, it soon transpired, had a crossed line with the instrument being used by the *Times* correspondent. All in all, it was a day which taught me a little about the pressures under which the touring media sometimes have to operate.

When the weather was at its worst, on the second scheduled day of the Test, Bourda was surrounded by a moat. It was an unbelievable sight, especially with various journalists having to peel off shoes and socks, hitch up their trousers and wade through the water to reach the sanctuary of the press box and the telephones which, nine times out of ten, did not work anyway.

I heard any number of theories expounded as to why it had rained so fiercely, ranging from the proximity of the new moon to a rather more romantic story concerning the removal of a statue of Queen Victoria from the city centre to the suburbs. Legend has it that cricket in Georgetown has been subjected to a curse ever since. Whatever the meteorological cause, I felt very sorry for the people. They had supported the one-day game in their thousands, many hanging from the trees outside the ground simply to gain some sort of view. They deserved a decent Test match. They were given nothing.

Instead of accompanying the England team to Trinidad, where they were due to play a four-day game in the oilfields of Pointe-à-Pierre, I had taken a week's leave from my duties for a proper holiday in Antigua. There, I had arranged to stay with some good friends, Bill and Elsa Cooper, and have a relaxing break with the new lady in my life, Thorunn. First, though, I had to get out of Georgetown, which proved unexpectedly difficult.

I had arrived at the airport deliberately early for my LIAT flight to Barbados and the preliminaries were smooth enough. Indeed, I was sitting on the plane before the problems began. It transpired that the Guyanan prime minister, Mr Greene, was also booked on the flight but, embarrassingly for someone, had not come with the correct travel document. The upshot was that the remainder of the passengers had to sweat it out for an hour, first on board and then on the tarmac, while the paperwork was concluded to everyone's satisfaction.

The delay was frustrating, but Antigua was worth the wait. It was a genuine holiday, free from all the myriad worries which had engulfed the preceding months of my life. I felt, for the first time in a long while, utterly at ease with myself, my company and my surroundings. Indeed, with Antigua being conspicuously short of daily newspapers, it was disarmingly easy for me to forget that I was still on a major cricket tour, with some pressing commitments to discharge. Come the end of my week in paradise, I flew on to Trinidad with a bit of catching up to do before the start of a Test match which, from my unaccustomed vantage point, was compulsive viewing from start to finish.

The natural temptation, which many felt unable to resist, had been to dismiss the Jamaica Test as a fluke. Many people, quite justifiably, suspected that England could not play as well again but that the West Indies could play a great deal better, especially with the bat. It was generally assumed that retribution was close at hand; instead, but for the cruellest strokes of ill fortune, England would have won again.

Before further bemoaning the fates, however, it is only balanced to report that England enjoyed a vital piece of good luck before the game began when they won the toss. There are some Tests in which a captain is quite ambivalent about the toss and others in which there is a clear advantage in having the choice. Seldom have I known a game where the first-day anticipation built to its climax not for the bowling of the opening over, but for the flicking of the coin.

As had always been likely, especially with the series at 1 – 0 in England's favour, the pitch had been left extremely well grassed. It was also damp. A cynical view has it that, in order to provide a surface which has a chance of surviving five days, the Trinidad authorities decree that an extra quota of water and grass are needed at the outset, which normally means that the game does not last those five days. Indeed, with the West Indies 29 for 5 before lunch, those who wished to back the draw were availing themselves of some very long odds, without any realistic hopes of collecting winnings.

No Test match should have such a high importance invested in the toss of a coin. It is a mockery of the five-day fundamental, which is essentially that the best team will usually win over such a long period providing conditions are fair and even. Having said that, it is a truism that bad pitches very often

*Ezra Moseley struck the vital blows on a
dramatic final day*

He hit Graham Gooch twice on the same spot on the left hand. His agony needs no description

produce riveting cricket. This was a marvellous match, fluctuating in a way which seemed improbable once England had taken the top five West Indies wickets for a pittance.

Devon Malcolm bowled furiously fast from his very first ball. Greenidge did not survive the over. Then the steady, skilful men Fraser and Small took two wickets each. Richards was absent, nursing a recurrence of his piles problem, but the best salvage man in the business was back in the side and in the sort of crisis which habitually inspires him. Gus Logie is one of those players who seem immeasurably more effective when the score is 29 for 5 than they are when it is 329 for 5. He is a street-fighting batsman. He plays everything very late, with a negligible backlift, and relies heavily on the sharpness of his eyes. When the bat comes through it all appears to be happening in a rush, no elegance but highly effective. He has been an irritant to England for years and it was a surprise to nobody that here, on his home ground, he was the originator of the West Indies' recovery. Logie stayed more than four hours and made 98, virtually half the West Indies total. He richly deserved a hundred but, having farmed the strike as, agonisingly for England, the last two wickets added 96, he cut a rare long hop from Fraser straight to cover. All too often, there is no justice in this game.

England's priority now was to achieve as large a lead as possible, and Gooch's instructions were clearly that time should not be thought a consideration. As a result, having progressed quickly to 43 without loss by the close of the first day, England spent all the second day adding only another 146, with Larkins and Stewart the casualties. Hindsight can be a great enemy to fair comment, and the outcome of the game prompted any number of wise-after-the-event remarks criticising Graham for not scoring more quickly. The more realistic assessment is that England would have lost the match but for the captain's six-hour 84.

The lead was 89, useful but not decisive, and when Greenidge and Haynes put on 96 for the first wicket as West Indies batted again, it seemed that all the advantage had been surrendered. Then came a pivotal passage of play, Fraser dismissing Greenidge before Malcolm, who had been thoroughly unimpressive, took three wickets within four balls of the next over. From 96 without loss, West Indies were 100 for 4, and this time even Logie could not halt the slide. They were all out, early on the final day, for 239, leaving England needing 151.

It sounds easy, of course – small target, plenty of time. But everything went wrong. Not at first, though, because for almost an hour England were making positive progress in the hands of Gooch and Larkins. It was the advent of Moseley which first knocked the day off its prescribed course. His first over took Larkins' wicket and, although nobody knew it at the time, broke Gooch's hand. If the first was a setback for England, the second was the single most telling blow of the entire series.

Gooch batted on, in considerable pain but unaware of the extent of his injury. Moseley's next over cut short his heroics. He hit him again in exactly the same spot, just above the knuckle of the left hand, and the many newspaper photographs of the impact tell of the agony. Graham went off to the local hospital, a stone's throw from Queen's Park Oval, where the hand was X-rayed. A serious fracture was shown but, being the man he is in the position he was, Graham decided that neither his own players nor, more pertinently, the opposition should be told of his incapacity until the game was over. He confided in the team management and in his vice-captain, but otherwise made light of it all to the point of padding up again as if preparing to resume his innings. It was a brave but ultimately futile gesture, foiled more than anything by weather so unseasonal as to be almost beyond belief.

Stewart and Lamb, who replaced Gooch, had both been playing forthright shots in the remaining overs of the morning. Stewart had found his efforts at crease-occupation unrewarding and made a conscious decision to have a full go whenever the ball was short. It was wonderful to watch – unless you happened to be the West Indies captain. What Haynes needed above all else was for his bowlers to make England work for the runs, with a tight line and fullish length. Instead, the bowling was short and reckless; even allowing for Gooch's demise it seemed that England would be home before tea-time.

Then the rain came. Slowly at first, but increasing in intensity to a point where one wondered just what the umpires hoped to achieve by allowing play to continue. With lunch imminent, the logical step would have been to take the players off, bring forward the interval and hope the weather allowed a prompt start. By persisting through several minutes of heavy rain, they allowed the pitch to take in more moisture and the outfield to become saturated so that when, eventually, the plastic covers were dragged out, across wet grass, they produced a greenhouse effect on the playing surface.

For some time we all thought it would be no more than a heavy shower. The sky around the ground even began to brighten – or so it seemed. Then it all filled in, like Manchester in November, teeming down as if it never meant to stop. Quite how it felt to be an England player in the dressing

Tensions rise on the last day in Trinidad –
normally Lamb and Haynes exchange rather
more pleasant words!

room, gazing at a scoreboard which read 73 for 1 and seeing an unthinkable 2 – 0 margin vanishing before your eyes, I can only guess. Even the press box was depressed.

Play did finally resume, but not until five minutes past four. The umpires calculated, heaven knows how, that 30 overs remained to be bowled which theoretically gave England every chance of making the remaining 77 runs required. In practice, England were battling the impending dusk, with the West Indies disinclined to help them. Some of the time-wasting gamesman-ship which ensued was plain ridiculous and had no place on a Test-match ground. England's frustration remained short of anger only for the know-ledge that, with roles reversed, they would have adopted similar tactics, if not quite so shamelessly.

With darkness falling fast and Walsh and Bishop bowling mercilessly fast, only the West Indies could win if the contest continued to its conclusion. England reluctantly accepted the draw to save life and limb. Call it a travesty. Maybe. It was certainly wholly unsatisfactory. The extra worry was that it would give the West Indies a double boost, saving a match and im-mobilising Gooch. Which, to my great surprise, is where I came into the reckoning.

CHAPTER ELEVEN

A Twist in the Tale

Let me make one thing clear from the outset. When I agreed to spend a couple of months on the Caribbean tour as a member of the media, the last thing I was anticipating, much less coveting, was that I would belatedly be recruited to the team. It did not enter my head that this was a serious possibility, partly because there were, as usual, designated standby players who had kept themselves fit all winter in case of emergencies, but largely because to summon me from the press-box would require a wholesale change of policy. Or so it seemed to me.

It is a popular theory, not publicly confirmed by anyone with inside information, that the principle reason for omitting me from the tour party concerned matters other than my personal fitness. It is said that I was left out because my perceived attitude towards training, preparation and general physical commitment would not sit comfortably with the new regime under Gooch and Stewart. If this was true, if indeed I was sacrificed for being an 'old lag' who had no place in a brave new world, then I could hardly hope to be whisked away from my notepad and telephone at the first hint of a crisis.

I was perfectly content with the welcome I had received from everyone in the West Indies, and perfectly resigned to the prospect of having to work harder than ever before, and probably make more runs than ever, if I was to resume my England career. This did not disturb me; on the contrary, I had come to see it as a driving incentive, so you may imagine my bewilderment on being asked to forget all previous instructions and come to the aid of the party.

It happened on that anguished final day of the Third Test in Trinidad. I was sitting in the BBC commentary box at the end of play, composing a few sad words for my newspaper column, when a message was delivered from the pavilion across the far side of the ground. Graham Gooch wished to see me urgently. At first I suspected something frivolous, such as Goooch and Lamb enquiring into the possibilities of a decent dinner venue at which to drown their sorrows. I did not, at the time, know the extent of Graham's hand injury; even if I had, I would have remained utterly unprepared for what was to follow.

I strolled across, as asked, and presented my compliments and commiserations to the skipper. He was, I thought immediately, a crestfallen sight, and once he had told me of the broken bones I could appreciate why. Brave public front or not, Graham was plainly struggling to play again on the cluttered climax to a tour he had done so much to inspire. It was a devastating blow for England and an unkind setback for him personally. I sympathised, still unaware of my part in the scheme of things.

The hierarchy was present in force, but it was Graham who asked the startling question. Was I fit? If so, would I be prepared to play in the three-day weekend game against Barbados? Quite apart from the injury situation, there were apparently a couple of players who the management believed must have a rest before the next Test, and although an official replacement for Graham was to be called, he could not be expected to arrive in time to play in a match scheduled to start in a little more than thirty-six hours.

Whether or not my expression betrayed my feelings I cannot say, but it is a fact that I was shocked. There were many aspects to consider. To begin with, I had not so much as held a bat since last September, apart from one bored afternoon in Georgetown when I had wandered unwittingly into an England practice session on the hotel tennis court and faced up to a few throw-downs from fifteen yards. I could hardly claim to be scrupulously prepared for a quick return to the big time. Set against all these doubts was an undeniable surge of excitement at the suggestion. My heart was pounding rather faster than usual. It was a very tempting proposal, but I forced myself to be realistic and professional about it. There was no telling what sort of pitch we might encounter in Barbados but, against their bowling, it was sure to be a stern test. I needed to have a proper net and assess my touch and fitness before finally committing myself.

What was very plain, even at this preliminary stage, was that Graham and Allan Lamb were keen that I should play. Micky Stewart raised no objections but I had the impression that he was doing no more than going along with the idea so long as it did not compromise stated policies. Later developments confirmed this to be the case.

Once we had broken up, following my agreement to join the boys for a serious net session the following afternoon, Graham had a private word with me. He was anxious in case I still felt a sense of resentment over the original squad selection, and told me he did not want me to reflect on it because things were different now that the team was enjoying some success. I replied that the issue was dead and buried and that my only concern, in this

Borrowed kit and a net in Barbados – the lack of helmet denotes that this was a gentle reintroduction to the game

unexpected situation, was being in the right shape to do myself and the team justice. Graham, comfortingly, repeated that it was down to me, and that if I did not feel up to it, nobody would think any the worse of me.

I retreated from Queen's Park Oval that evening in something of a turmoil. Obliged to keep the new circumstances confidential, I pondered alone on the possibilities. Naturally, I had to seek some advice and I phoned my manager, Jon Holmes, in Nottingham, whose sound verdict was that I should retain control of my destiny and not allow myself to be pushed into anything for which I was not ready.

By the following morning, when the playing party and press gathered at Piarco Airport for the flight to Barbados, the rumours had spread fast. Some were grossly exaggerated, as inevitably happens, and I quietly had to explain that there was no question, at least at this stage, of my being required for either of the last two Test matches. I had been asked to help out against Barbados and that was the extent of the proposed involvement. I was telling

Thanks for the game! Time to join Hampshire's practice after a disappointing game against Barbados

the absolute truth, but I don't suppose I wholly convinced anyone. The press knew, as well as I did, that if I played in the three-day match, and happened to make a big score, there would be a very good case for considering me for the Test team. But it was not going to be me who voiced the possibility.

Prospective player or not, I remained a journalist at this juncture, with a few final commitments to *The Times*. And so it was that, seated on the crowded flight, I balanced my writing pad on my knee and set about the curious assignment of writing a piece about my own recall.

Once in Barbados, I had a brief chat with Graham and Allan in the arrivals hall, then changed identity again and took a taxi to the beachside hotel where the press were staying, a mile or so from the team hotel. I phoned my copy, had a light and slightly nervy lunch and then set off to Kensington Oval to reacquaint myself with the theory of batting.

It was never likely to be a private workout and, sure enough, the area behind the net pitches was healthily populated both with journalists eager for a story and with English tourists, over for the cricket and doubtless mystified by my presence in the net. Somebody wittily cracked that it was the biggest turnout to watch an England net since the one I infamously decreed to be 'optional' on England's last West Indian tour!

I batted for the best part of an hour, primarily against Gladstone Small. In assessing how it went I had two priorities: firstly, I must have no reaction from my shoulder, or it would simply not be worth the risk of aggravating the injury; and secondly, I wanted to feel in reasonable touch, without expecting mid-season timing at the first attempt. I was totally satisfied on the first point and not unhappy about the second. After another, briefer knock the following morning, I agreed to give it a go.

In Graham's absence, 'Lamby' took over as captain. Great friend though he is, I have to say that he did me few favours on this occasion. When he won the toss, he chose to field first on the basis that the Barbados pitch is often at its liveliest on the first morning. Given the make-up of our side, with a second-string attack but a number of batsmen needing time in the middle (self included), this was definitely not a good idea.

I knew I was capable of doing the job before me. Of course I did. What I needed was to get out there and rediscover *how* to do it. This would have been best served by batting on the first day, when the wicket was at its best and my adrenalin was at its highest. It was not to be. We had a largely unprofitable day in the field while two of the Barbados Test players, Greenidge and Best, took the chance of some welcome practice. Greenidge made 183, Best 95. At close of play they were 340 for 4 and I wondered if I would even get in on the second day.

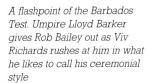

A flashpoint of the Barbados Test. Umpire Lloyd Barker gives Rob Bailey out as Viv Richards rushes at him in what he likes to call his ceremonial style

As things turned out I was in soon after lunch – despite batting at number six. Our spinners took the remaining six Barbados wickets inside an hour, and then Malcolm Marshall, who had missed the Trinidad Test through injury, gave himself a tick on the Fourth Test selection sheet with some skilful swing and seam bowling at three-quarter pace. We were in something of a pickle when I went in and, although I managed to hang around for forty minutes or so, we were little better off when I took my leave with a mere 4 runs to my name.

My nerves had been jangling while I waited to bat but, having got out in the middle, I felt comfortably relaxed. Marshall and the other seamers ensured that it was far from being a gentle reintroduction, and I was aware of being not quite in touch. I was feeling for the ball a shade deliberately rather than waiting for it and reacting instinctively. Frustratingly, though, I was just getting the hang of it when I got out, turning a ball off my legs with the middle of the bat only to see it fly straight to a fielder who had craftily been brought into square leg for the purpose.

We were bowled out more than 200 behind, despite a good innings from

Nasser Hussain with his thus far unconfirmed broken wrist. Predictably, however, Desmond Haynes did not enforce the follow-on, which would have given us a valuable chance to redeem ourselves, and nor did he make an early declaration on the final day. In fact, he made no effort to win the game at all, delaying his token declaration until mid-afternoon. They were curious tactics if one was concerned solely with the possibility of Barbados scoring another victory over a touring team, but I had never expected Desmond's thinking to be so single-minded. He was concerned more with the remaining Test matches and knew that he had scored another psychological point if he deprived us of the opportunity to get batsmen into form.

For me, it was a deflating end to the game as I did not get in at all in the second innings. My output for the game was well below what was necessary to justify an extension of the experiment and we reverted to the original plan, which meant me joining up with the Hampshire squad who had now arrived on the island, while agreeing to stand by in case of further emergencies.

This, of course, was the way it had to be. There could be no argument about that. David Smith had now arrived, after what seemed a tortuous procedure of selection, organisation and travel, to deputise for the captain, and with fit players from the existing tour party available, it would not have been diplomatically clever even to hint that I might be included in the Test.

It had not been a wasted exercise for me. I had, in a funny way, enjoyed my time in the field and discovered from it precisely how much work I still needed to do on my body before the English season began. Similarly, although I did not make many runs, the innings did restore some self-confidence in my ability to bat without pain from my shoulder. And, as important to me as anything else, I had slotted back into the dressing room atmosphere without apparent unease from any direction, strange though it seemed to be there almost in the guise of the old-fashioned part-timer.

There was, in any case, no time to feel any sense of disappointment. It was my birthday, and despite the fact that it was a Sunday and we were on a Caribbean island, we managed to summon a good supply of high-quality champagne at a French restaurant and celebrate the event in some style. I felt a little old, a little tired and just a shade emotional by the end of a long evening. The next day, my journalistic duties having ended, I left the comparative luxury of the Grand Barbados Hotel for the spartan but functional Woodville Apartments, Hampshire's base for their two-week pre-season tour.

It demanded a substantial adjustment. Thorunn had gone home; I was no longer a media person; I was no longer an England player. In fact, I was cooking my own eggs, brewing my own coffee and getting acquainted with the men who were to be my new team-mates, some of them so totally new to me that genuine introductions were called for.

I had not been the new boy in a dressing room for many years and it was, at first, a strange feeling, accentuated by the fact that most of the Hampshire boys I knew pretty well were elsewhere – Robin Smith with England, Marshall with the West Indies and Mark Nicholas languishing in the Queen Elizabeth Hospital with malaria. Poor Mark had only transited in London on returning from the England A tour in Zimbabwe. He caught a connecting flight to Barbados to link up with his county, but began to feel unwell on the plane and needed to call for oxygen. He admitted himself to hospital during his first night on the island and malaria was confirmed the following day. He was, for a time, in a pretty bad way, and in his absence the tour was run by Tim 'Trooper' Tremlett, who is now captain of the second team.

After a couple of nets, I played my first match for Hampshire in the unlikely setting of the Barbados Police ground. We arrived early, and were rather taken aback to be asked if we would mind starting in ten minutes, because there was a football match to be played as soon as we had finished! Amusing though this sounds, it cost me dear. The advanced start meant that I did not have adequate time to devote to stretching exercises, which are important at all times but vital when you are thirty-three years old and have a winter's inactivity to overcome. The first time I chased a ball in the field, I felt a thigh muscle tweak.

I did not move well for the rest of the Police innings and although I could bat easily enough, and scored 50-odd, it was an irritating injury which inhibited me for the next few days and was to recur back in England, discounting me from the first couple of games in the new season. It was not the start for which I would have wished.

While continuing to net each day with Hampshire, I was able to watch the last half of each day's play in the Barbados Test match, in between looking up some old friends and making the most of the ample social facilities the island has to offer.

That England were up against it was apparent before the start. Losing Gooch was bad enough, but the situation became critical when Fraser, their steadiest bowler, suffered an intercostal injury which was to rule him out of the last two Tests. There was also a cruel stroke of fortune for David Smith, who had his thumb injured (much later it was found to be broken) in his first innings of the trip. Like Gooch, whom he had replaced, his tormentor was Ezra Moseley. Smith, too, was out of the Test and the tour, while the West Indies were able to name a full-strength team for the first time in the series. It did not look, indeed did not turn out to be, a pitch of any great pace or venom, but in my heart I feared for England, and with good reason.

*England were finally beaten by Curtly
Ambrose's spell of five for 18 on the last
evening*

They were beaten, but not without a titanic struggle which took the game well into its final hour. The eventual margin of 165 runs was possibly a fair reflection of the difference between the teams on this occasion but, having come so close and been so cruelly denied in Port of Spain, it was a form of rough justice now for England to come within half an hour of saving the game and still fail. It was a game of some controversy, with warnings issued for short-pitched bowling and Viv Richards showing such animation at the fall of English wickets that some observers considered he was trying to intimidate the umpires.

I saw some of Allan Lamb's second hundred of the series and, as when watching his first during the win in Jamaica, felt the same confusing mix of emotions. I was pleased for a friend, pleased for England, but regretful that I was not out there with the chance to make runs on what, apart from the occasional ball keeping low, was a belter of a pitch.

But on any pitch against West Indian bowling, a century needs hard work and concentration. You are still earmarked for some unpleasant balls, the more the longer you stay, and runs never come easily and seldom quickly against their relentless fast bowling.

For 'Lamby', the pleasure may have been diminished by the defeat, but it must equally have been increased by this being his first Test as captain. A.J. Lamb is not, and never has been, the likeliest character to lead England. There are those, like myself, whose names are filed from an early age as potential captains and who often spend far too long having to live up to the expectation. There are others, like Allan, for whom the job is a very much longer shot.

I am sure it never crossed his mind, until very recently, that he might end up in charge. But then he took over at Northamptonshire, and did well until a baffling and untypical spate of injuries ended his season early. He became intensely depressed by the injuries for the simple reason that he had always previously been fit, but when elevated to vice-captain of England on this trip he rose visibly to the challenge. He will never totally change, and nor should he. He is a born extrovert and it is this quality which decorates his cricket, lifting him above the ordinary. But he has reacted well to responsibility and has changed sufficiently, with the pips on his shoulders, to command a high degree of respect from the lads.

From my own observations during my time on the tour, he revelled in his duties. Like Graham Gooch, however, he is not a great orator, so he has to set his example on the field, and specifically through his batting. On this tour, it was not a problem to him. He seems to thrive against West Indian bowling – witness his three centuries against them in 1984 and another in 1988 – and I honestly believe he is still improving as a Test player at the rare old age of thirty-five.

'Lamby' did not emerge from his captaincy baptism totally unscathed. He was criticised for putting the West Indies in to bat, and as they made 446 it is hard to argue his case. He was also criticised, on the fourth day, for slowing down the game almost as blatantly, if not as theatrically, as Haynes had done in Trinidad. Haynes, who was batting at the time, actually clapped Lamb off the field at lunch, a sardonic recognition of 15 – all.

As I did not see all this conscious inactivity I am not best placed to comment, but I will say that the 90-overs minimum is unrealistic in the West Indies, where the temperatures are high, drinks breaks are frequent and daylight hours are short. It can, as we saw twice during this series, become a totally cynical operation when the fielding side is under pressure, because the captain can slow things down in the knowledge that play cannot possibly continue past six o'clock. As I am against a fining system, which I simply do not believe to be the answer, I can only suggest that a slower and more attainable number of overs in a day should be specified on future

Graham Gooch, unable to take part in the last two Tests, is left to reflect on what might have been

tours to avoid such farcical scenes.

So there it was. The series was poised at 1 – 1, with one to play, and I was poised to go home. I had enjoyed my time, unexpected diversions notwithstanding. I had learned from the experience and, I think, I had coped. As a first exercise in combining writing and broadcasting I was happy with it, and although I do not see it as a lifetime's work, I was encouraged to do more. The writing and transmitting was totally new to me but I managed the mechanics of it without too much stress; the broadcasting demanded different disciplines, but giving my views off the cuff, making mistakes and correcting them was a stimulating challenge.

There had, when it all began, been some scope for uncomfortable moments in the press box, among some characters for whom I have little time or respect. There were times when it felt strange to be working in the company of men whose poisonous pens had given me such a miserable summer as England captain, but this was not a general grievance. I got on well with most of the cricket writers and if there were some with whom I would not have chosen to spend time – indeed, a few of whom I will remain eternally suspicious – this is also the case in cricket and, probably, every other walk of life. I saw at first hand the problems encountered in meeting deadlines against a difficult time difference. I came away with a greater understanding of it, but, on balance, I have to say it is easier than playing.

The Barbados Test ended on a Tuesday evening and the players were to fly on to Antigua later that night prior to the start of the final Test on the Thursday. My schedule with Hampshire involved another couple of games and a flight home to London on the Friday, but once again my plans were changed at the request of the England management. With the doubt about David Smith's thumb persisting, and various other batsmen carrying minor, niggling injuries, they asked me to accompany the side to Antigua and stand by to play in the decisive Test.

My thigh had recovered, my shoulder felt good and, with a couple of match innings and a series of net sessions behind me, I was confident that I could do myself justice if called upon. Antigua being a favourite island of mine, and the pitch traditionally being batsman-friendly, I travelled in hope and expectation.

It was late when we checked into the Renaissance Hotel, in one of Antigua's lovely bays. In fact it was past two in the morning and it was difficult to comprehend that another Test match was scheduled for the following day. Absurd scheduling, or strict necessity? The arguments could rage for ever on that one but it is a fact that the English season was to begin before the party returned home. There was to be no rest now, and certainly none when the tour ended. I felt suddenly relieved that I, for one, would be starting the

Robin Smith hit on the jaw by Courtney Walsh
during a torrid innings which also left him
with a broken finger – and he says he loves it

season relatively fresh.

Practice on Wednesday was restricted, for the very good reason that most players needed a break. Jack Russell looked drained by his efforts in Barbados, which climaxed in a five-hour defensive innings of such tenacity that it almost saved the match. Others, too, were showing the effects, physical and mental, of a daunting schedule. In hindsight, the indicators for what was to follow were all too clear.

I had various chats that day with Messrs Lamb and Gooch. They were seeking signs of confidence from me, and I think they got them. I received the distinct impression that Lamb, who would be captaining the side again, was very keen that I should play, even if it was ahead of a fit member of the squad.

Sleep was fitful that night. I kept turning over in my head the situation in which I now found myself. I was excited by the prospect of resuming my Test career in such an atmosphere. By the morning I had built myself up to the job at hand. No one had officially told me I was playing but I knew I was ready.

West Indies have won the series, just before the rain came. The presentation ceremony was damp, but no less celebratory

We were half an hour from the scheduled start when the deflating news was broken to me. I was knocking up with Rob Bailey on the far side of the ground while the management held a lengthy conference in the middle. I could guess the subject of their discussion and it was confirmed when, as one, they turned to walk toward me, the captain expressionless at their head.

I had been left out. It was close, apparently very close, but the selection had hinged on the belief that established policies would be weakened if, at the very end of a successful tour, someone was left out to accommodate a player who had not originally been chosen. There were enough fit players so there was no pressing reason to include me.

I could see the point. Of course I could. Had I been Nasser Hussain, or Rob Bailey, I would not have been very impressed at losing my place to an outsider after all the effort put in over three months. But from a purely personal viewpoint I admit to feeling unaccountably disappointed. I had built up my hopes and they had been dashed. Now, all I could do was try to rearrange my journey home while England fought a hopeless battle for survival against a side with confidence restored.

By flying back to Barbados and linking up again with Hampshire, I arrived back in London on Saturday, which, back in Antigua, was the nadir of the entire England tour. Bowled out for 260, they then conceded 228 runs in 51 overs without dividing Greenidge and Haynes. They rallied the following day, but the game was beyond them and the end was swift and clinical. As England were dismissed for 148 on the fourth day, and beaten by an innings and plenty, it transpired that both Hussain and Robin Smith had been batting with broken bones. In Hussain's case, he had gone into the game with a fractured wrist. Perhaps, after all, they had needed me. But I have to be honest – the cricket I saw on the television of that game did suggest that I was far safer sitting on the BA flight home than attempting to have a net in the middle of that Test match!

Such thought did not linger. Back in England, I had to find somewhere to live and estalbish myself in my new cricketing home with Hampshire. It was the new start I had planned, the new environment I needed. A crazy, cluttered year of confused emotions lay behind me. An entirely fresh challenge lay ahead.